THE HAPPY DOG BOOK

Forepaw-word. This open, frank and honest exposé represents a communications breakthrough, revealing for the first time our desires, frustrations, aspirations and downright filthy and disgusting habits.

Proud to be off the leash, the canine community trots out of the closet, with heads held low (in case there's something interesting to sniff), in this sensational straight-barking, language-busting canine confessional. Having said that, this is a deeply serious work which will go a long way to heal 'interspecies rift' and promote 'interspecies understanding'. Furthermore, young pups can learn a thing or two from us gruff, hard-bitten, long in the tooth, old dogs of the world.

It is our belief that humans can't see in colour properly. For humanitarian reasons therefore, we offer this volume in black and white.

Oh, I almost forgot. Ian Fleming is a freelance advertising and graphic design consultant and writer. He lives in central London.

Your four-footed friend,
'Tyrannosaurus' Rex (Editor)

'Damn it! He's found my dentures again.'

1

ACKNOWLEDGEMENTS

CONTRIBUTORS Cartoonists

Ken Allen
David Austin
Les Barton
Bek
Philip Berkin
Nick Baker
Jim Hunter
Tony Husband
Martin Honeysett
Sidney Harris
Richard Jolley
Russell Jones

Neil Kerber
David Myers
Dean Moore
Giles Pilbrow
Rupert Redway
Adam Singleton
Geoff Thompson
Robert Thompson
Nicholas Whitmore
Kipper Williams
Bob Wilson
Gerald Whyman

Australian National Kennel Council
Pam Gardner (dog hair garment designer)
01327 350025
Mr & Mrs John Davis (Sparky's owners)

BIBLIOGRAPHY & PERMISSIONS

British Rate & Data
Concise Encyclopedia of Dogs
(Octopus Books)
Dogs Today Magazine
Dogs Monthly Magazine
Dog Watching, Desmond Morris
(Jonathan Cape)
Dog World Newspaper
House & Garden Magazine
The Illustrated Encyclopedia of Dogs
(Quarto Publishing)
Mikki Pet Products Ltd
The Intelligence of Dogs, Stanley Coren
(Headline)
National Enquirer, European edition

Our Dogs Newspaper
Private Eye Magazine
Punch Ltd
The Sons of the Desert, Helpmate Tent
The Spectator, Michael Heath
The Daily Telegraph Newspaper
The Dog's Mind, Bruce Fogle
(Pelham Books)
Why Does My Dog..., John Fisher
(Bantam Books)
Your Dog Magazine

PRODUCTION

Downtown Photo Laboratory, Steve Walsh
Joe's Basement Photo Laboratory
Jon Morgan of Head (cover design)
Prontaprint, Brewer Street, London W1
Jon Rogers, Ian Fleming Associates Ltd
Jackie Grostate, Page make up

Original Photography pages 30,32,56,64.
Paul King Photography
Special thanks to Leila, Syndication Dept *House
& Garden,* and the following talented designers
whose work first appeared in it:
Sarah Charles   0171 370 6027
Stephen Calloway   0171 703 5009
Andre Dubreuil   0171 727 5531
Nicholas Hills   01328 700 700
Nicholas Haslam   0171 730 8623
Patrick Pender   01752 663785

'I know, everyone vill
be needing lots and
lots of zis...'

'We're not really
into reading
books'.

THE HAPPY DOG BOOK

BY IAN FLEMING
AND A PANEL OF EXPERT DOGS

HEADLINE

Copyright © Ian Fleming 1997

The right of Ian Fleming to be identified as the Author
of the Work has been asserted by him in acccordance with the
Copyright, Designs and Patents Act 1988.

First published in 1997
by HEADLINE BOOK PUBLISHING

10 9 8 7 6 5 4 3 2 1

Cataloguing in Publication Data is available from the British Library

ISBN 07472 2054 9

Designed and typeset by Ian Fleming
Edited by Susan Fleming

Printed and bound in Great Britain by
Mackays of Chatham PLC, Chatham, Kent

HEADLINE BOOK PUBLISHING
A division of Hodder Headline PLC
338 Euston Road
London NW1 3BH

CONTENTS

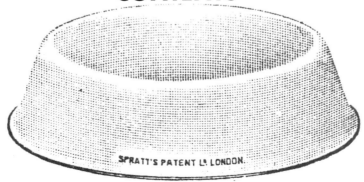

SPRATT'S PATENT Lᵈ LONDON.

INTRODUCTION

Working with a team of literary dogs has its rewards (mostly bones, admittedly), but now that Fleet Street has moved to the Isle of Dogs several miles from my studio in Soho, I found so often that my collaborators, 'Tyrannosaurus' Rex and his panel of paw-in-the-door newshounds and hungry packarazzi, were so often tied up in meetings discussings scraps of information, or even just scraps, that I was left very much on my own. By then I was bitten by the bug (fleas, I think), and plunged unmuzzled into the arcane world of the dog and his relationship with his owner.

There is no question that dogs enjoy a privileged place in the home, and provide their human pack with unswerving (unless they've been on the beer) loyalty, devotion and protection. But Professor Archer of The University of Central Lancashire finds pet ownership puzzling in evolutionary terms. It is a case of human beings, a member of one species, providing food and care for a member of another species (dogs, cats, alligators and what have you), when there is no apparent benefit to the provider. Now, that may be true of cats (sorry about that, you cats), but in these pages you will read of dogs that work tirelessly and enthusiastically at all manner of humanitarian tasks to earn their daily br...bones.

The good professor thinks that we are being manipulated by our pets to 'obtain benefits and form bonds producing mutually satisfying interactions'. Well, what is a poor pariah to do when his owner buys him anniversary cards, presents, personalised birthday cakes and even calls him on the phone during absences, like vacations? (Sounds like love to me.) The fact is that owners bestow human characteristics on their dogs, reinforced when Fido settles down to enjoy TV or when he sings along with the theme tune from Neighbours. Pretty soon he's on Easy Street (a place boasting a lamppost every ten metres). After all, every hound worth his salt lick possesses a full wardrobe from which to choose on his visits to the groomer for his weekly make-over. He must never be disturbed whilst sleeping on his owner's bed, and when he awakens, all he needs to do is to display interest in, say, prime beef tartare, et voilà, life is cracked, along with several juicy bones. Farewell, daily grind (unless it's bones). A life of ease, comfort and distraction awaits amongst his cupboard full of toys.

The generally accepted theory is that all dogs are descended from wolves. Wolves live in packs practising a strict hierarchical family structure, the better to control the essential tasks of hunting, mating and rearing cubs. The leader is called the alpha male - the top dog to whom all others kow tow. According to Palaeolithic rock paintings, man first tamed dogs 10,000 years ago, then used, trained and bred dogs to perform specific tasks related to survival, like hunting, food gathering and retrieval, guarding, vermin control and fighting (the dogs of war). The modern dog is seldom required to perform these sorts of duties and often lives a solitary life in the home. He never loses his basic instincts though, and our perception of how the mind of a dog works is based entirely on his 'wolvine' origins.

Researchers at Southampton University's Anthrozoology Institute discovered that toy and lapdog breeds behave like puppies (aka wolf cubs) all their lives as a result of selective breeding. They retain immature characteristics affecting their independence and predictability. They have much in common with our human babies, big eyes, short limbs, snubby nose, cute hair (see page 90), and we like them that way – because they are babyish. Owners even talk baby-speak to them. It may well account for a King Charles Spaniel called Lotte who saw it as her mission in life to clear all pavements and paths of dog-ends. Something any self-respecting one-year-old baby would relate to.

And talking of puppyish, some of the book is a bit that way, but then it was written to teach them a thing or two. They can always turn to the more 'adult' sections, as can my homo sapiens readers, but enough of all that. It's hard to get too serious about critters who snack on fox poo and 'pavement pizzas'.

Based on dogged canine research, everything in this book is sort of true-ish (OK, I lied about Viper's-Bugloss on page 113, it really should never be anally inserted into a human). This book's real purpose is to trot over to the seamier, smuttier, shadier side of the street, taking care to turn off well before the world of Crufts Dog Show, as it were, in order to bite the odd postman and scare the wits out of that pedigree Persian cat. In other words (and you'll soon wish they were other words), it's not the kind of stuff you'll find in any other dog book.

I can best describe the (literary?) content, in terms of a perfect dog day out. First, a good run around chasing ball, frisbee or stick. Then a deep refreshing draught of lavatory bowl water, followed by a pint at the pub, whilst exploring the upper regions of a lady's skirt from the inside. Then, upon sniffing a bitch on heat, a couple of hours mating in front of the local Presbyterian Church on Sunday morning. All that, after having seen off the competition in a vicious dog fight. A bit peckish by now, some ripe kippers from the garbage can will do nicely before rolling in a putrified, squelchy, sea gull carcass in mud, and then a well-deserved sleep on the newly laundered white eiderdown at home. It doesn't sound a bad life does it, and to a dog this is of course perfectly normal behaviour, in the best possible taste.

Yes, all is revealed, no bone unturned. 'Tyrannosaurus' was complimentary and calls me an honorary dog, or was it ornery dog? I daren't ask, he's one of those irascible 'bite much, much, much worse than his bark', individuals.

IAN FLEMING

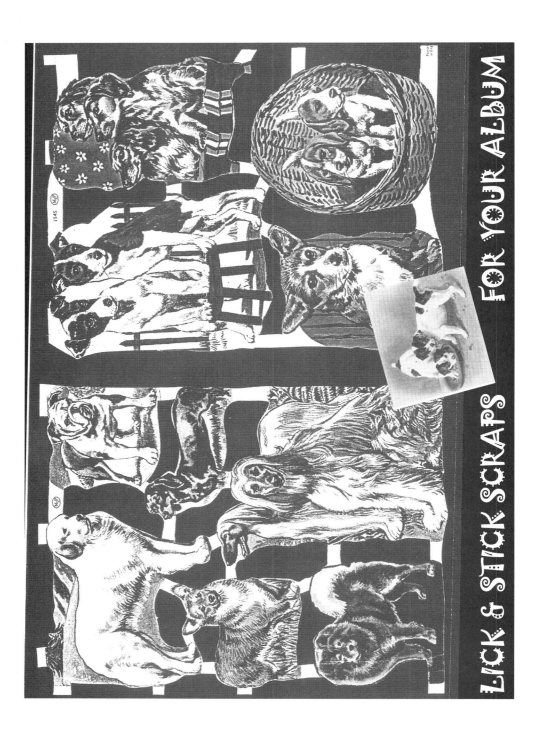

8

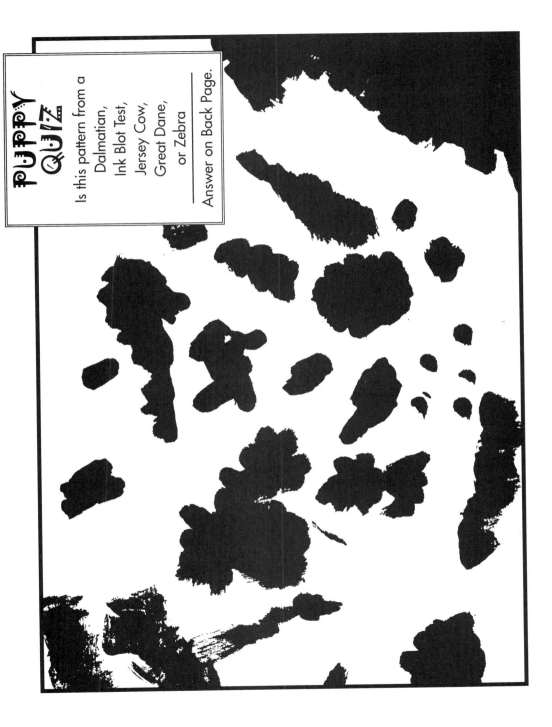

PUPPY QUIZ

Is this pattern from a
Dalmatian,
Ink Blot Test,
Jersey Cow,
Great Dane,
or Zebra

Answer on Back Page.

Favourite Lampposts and other street furniture

A sniffer dog writes

WHY LAMPPOSTS AND TREES?
Sadly many dogs live alone, often in apartments with no gardens. The only opportunity to meet other dogs is the daily walk. 'Meet' is a loose term here because olfactory information centres, as we dogs call street furniture and trees, offer a chance to leave a business card and to access a library of information through our amazing sense of smell (see 'Why Dogs are Superior to Humans' on page 108) which is 250,000 times greater than humans. We can form a district dog map: we can identify how many animals have used the facility, at what frequency, the sex, breed, age, and at what time of day. Not bad eh...for a dog.

But it's actually more than that. It is equivalent to a dating agency or notices in the cornershop. Our territorial markings are essential so that other dogs can read our messages by detecting our pheromones.

LAMPPOSTS
In a recent survey published here, the Victorian four-sided cast-iron base type was preferred because;

1. Four sides offer more surface area.
2. Two or more dogs can sniff around at the same time.
3. Allows longer 'lingering time' to absorb and analyse information.
4. Better to detect competition or new boys on the block.

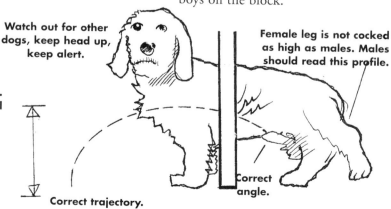

Watch out for other dogs, keep head up, keep alert.

When sniffing, allow for dog height differentials. Yorkies, with an all time record low of 6.3cms or 2½ inches (at the shoulder) as opposed to Great Danes 105cms or 40 inches tall.

Correct trajectory.

Female leg is not cocked as high as males. Males should read this profile.

Correct angle.

Concrete lampposts were unpopular. Often sited on busy dual carriageways, there is an element of danger in using them. Extremely unrelaxing and stressful.

POSTBOXES

Whilst we deplore the hole-in-the-wall types, free standing boxes were unanimously voted top favourites. The canine community congratulates the Post Office on their splendid oval First and Second Class type boxes. These offer a genuine meeting place where we can exchange information, but owing to problems outlined on page 82, an, ah hum, 'communications problem,' exists here.

BOLLARDS

The square-based type is infinitely preferable to the round. Good, but not quite so satisfactory as the Victorian lamppost, but not to be sniffed at, as it were.

TELEPHONE BOXES

Generally speaking to be avoided. Members report a high incidence of kicking and RUNS*. However if you are female, leave your 'calling card' (humans do). Something along the lines of *Attractive Bitch Seeks Generous Stud Dog for Watersports.'*

LITTER BINS

Examples in the Royal Parks and the Royal Borough of Kensington & Chelsea are top favourites amongst our pedigree members as well as Upwardly Mobile Mongrels (UMM's). You are likely to meet a better class of dog, although it is prudent to avoid corgis (you never know).

RECYCLING BINS

Tempting, but potentially fraught with danger for two reasons:
1. Broken glass around bottle banks
2. Paper banks provide potential for RUNS.*

METROPOLITAN DRINKING FOUNTAIN & CATTLE TROUGH ASSOCIATION

These magnificent watering opportunity sites are obsolete troughs for bovines and the like. Do not drink from them, the water is rank (but so are our coats very often), and they are full of litter.

*Rolled-Up Newspaper Syndrome (see page 36).

'Lovely evening for a stroll, darling...hold, on I'll just have another pee.'

We sent Smudger, our very own prince of the paparazzi (or is it the pavement pizza), to snap this photographic still-life essay of some of London's 'watering opportunity sites', proving that there is still life in the old dog yet.

METROPOLITAN DRINKING FOUNT

N & CATTLE TROUCH ASSOCIATION

Constructed of granite, they have a natural affinity with Scottish dogs. They also seem to act as a magnet for Dachshunds, who figure that they have been especially constructed for them, (but Dachshunds are not the brightest among us!).

OTHER STREET FURNITURE
Parking meters, street signage posts and dustbins should be avoided. Surface areas are insufficient. Wheelie bins and dustbins are frequently moved, but are often good for picking up fox scent.

'Cocker' Leakie calls for 'A tree in every garden and a lamppost on every corner.'

Useful Tips

- Wait around postboxes until collection time. Then 'fix' the postman's scent. You may want to bite him later.

- Don't hang around lampposts too long, especially at night. You may get a bad reputation, or worse, taken to the dog pound.

- Don't urinate on the lamppost electrics. Often the electrics door is missing. Check carefully.

- When you hit those mean streets, watch out for traffic and avoid street corner sites.

A New York fire hydrant and a London lamppost have been installed in the QE2's kennels so that both American and British dogs can feel at home.

The canine community votes with its feet in **THE HDB POLL** of Poles, Lampposts, Postboxes and Other Street Furniture.

Advanced metal fatigue and oxidisation has caused imminent collapse of this modern so-called 'fixture'. Traditional cast iron holds no danger of 'one-cocked leg-too-many' syndrome.

Favourite Trees

Generally speaking, the canine community prefers large old trees standing in public parks or streets. Ideally these should have a bark that is heavily creviced, fissured, gnarled and textured (just like an old mongrel I once mated with), to offer the best 'message absorption' qualities. Particularly recommended are common alder, sweet and horse chestnut, oak (especially cork oak), elm, lime, poplar, pear and pine. But what do these so-called sophisticated 'townie' dogs know? They're wasting their time with smooth-barked species like London plane, holly, beech and birch. This is because in wet weather our chemical signals are easily diluted.

Useful Tips

❧ Drink plenty of water before going out. Many animals run out of pee and are, as it were, caught short.

❧ Lots of females cock their legs instead of squatting, but less high than their male counterparts. Single dogs should watch out for this lowered profile.

❧ Be on guard against barbed wire imbedded in or around the trunk of trees. This can cause the unwary nasty wounds in sensitive places (not applicable to Wire haired Terriers).

❧ Staked pavement trees with small patches of earth are excellent scratch'n'sniff sites.

❧ Should your owner attempt to pull you away, react vigorously. In Paris, apparently the authorities have urination centres for humans situated on the pavements. These are called *pissoirs*. French poodles please note.

SORTING THE DOGWOOD FROM THE TREES
Some breeds and their favourites

Breed	Favourite
Alsation Police Dog	Copper Beech
Australian Sheep Dog	Eucalyptus
Bloodhound	Any staked tree
Boxer	Box tree
Boston Terrier	Tea Tree
Bearded Collie	Old Man's Beard
Chihuahua	Mexican Pine
Chi Tzu	Bonsai Tree
Chow Chow	Chinese Tulip Tree
Dachshund	Any it can Dachs to; low-slung tree
Dalmation	Black or White Poplars
Great Dane	Any non-splash-back tree
Jack Russell Terrier	Cricket Bat Willow
Japanese Spitz	Ornamental Cherry
King Charles Spaniel	Oak
Old English Sheepdog	Shagbark Hickory
Papillon Spaniel	Buddleia Butterfly Bush
Poodle	Lombardy Poplar
Red Setter	Giant Redwood
Saint Bernard	Mountain Ash
Staffordshire Bull Terrier	Any tree in a clay or glazed pot
Yorkshire Terrier	Cricket stumps (Willow)

NICHOLAS

A GUEST CAT WRITES

At home there is never a problem with Hamlet – he's a Great Dane with whom I, eh hum, cohabit. We've lived together (no, don't get me wrong) for five years now, and we get on together just fine. Most cats and dogs do, you know, despite what they say. It's in the garden that we have our 'contretoms'.

and us cats are the, as it were, catalysts. Predatory instincts, I hear you literate thoroughbreds ask? (If only mongrels could read.) I think not, because when they catch us they don't know what to do and let us off. Mind you, our 'fluffed-up tail, teeth and claw display' combined with blood-curdling screeching might have something to do with it. If it came to a dog fight, we're a teeny bit quicker than Mr Dog – we can use our claws seven times faster than he can even open his jaws.

I've come to the conclusion that dogs will chase anything that moves just for the fun of it. Squirrels, joggers, cyclists

It's just good fun for them, but 54 kg of Great Dane charging at 25 mph is not so amusing. What is a cat to do? Move very very fast is what. I might look asleep under that garden bench, but we cats need to be ever wary when we're catnapping. Off I set across the lawn, yowling and caterwauling, as you do, up the fence and in true cat-amongst-the-pigeons style, leap into the nearest tree and climb to the top.

He can bark up the right tree for as long as he wants but I tell you this, I've had enough. If the Fire Brigade don't come soon I'm moving next door. No-one owns us, we own territory is all, and its no coincidence that we cats are

FOR BRIGADE

ahead in the pet popularity stakes, because frankly, we're so much more civilised. Sorry about that, Hamlet, but if you miss me I'll be on the fence, but right now, if I had a cat-o'-nine-tails...

Why Humans Like 'Walkies' Twice a Day

Our keep-fit correspondent gets hot under the collar about physical jerks

Listen, we know things. We've worked out the real reason why we're dragged around the park twice a day. No, it's not for the exercise, not for the fresh air, and NOT for our benefit. Unmated owners use us as an introduction agency to meet the opposite sex. It makes me foam at the mouth the way we are blatantly exploited. We can tell, it's the pheromones you see, but you probably don't know about that stuff (see chapter on 'Why Dogs Are Superior to Humans').

A decent walk is impossible and frankly, it dogs our step to be brought to a throat choking halt every few yards when some likely lad or lass stops to ask personal questions about US – never the owner we note! Very flattering, I thought at first. All that patting, petting and attention, very solicitous, wag, wag. But solicit is the word I'd use now. They treat us like conversation pieces. 'What's his name? Artichoke eh, that's an unusual name, mine's called Tatty, and by the way my name is Hubert Bedfellow, how do you do.' Or it's, 'She's lovely, what breed is she? She's in fine condition, what do you give her to eat? My Spot won't eat chicken because of the bones.'

Walk the plank.

'A marvellous invention. It means you can let them wander about without the fear that they're going to get lost.'

22

The fact is we're rarely offered chicken and anyway, we're sitting here waiting for this heard-it-a-thousand-times-before-conversation to end. 'He knows every word I say,' as if I'm not there. OK, in that case, why don't you ask me? (But we forget, they don't speak Desperanto.) All that doggerel, makes you sick. Then they say 'See you tomorrow.' All very well, but it's us who do all the hard work, sniffing rumps and all that exploratory stuff we have to do. And what if you don't even like her stupid little Suzikins? If you growl you get half choked, if you sort of like her, *plutonically* that is, you're lumbered. 'Look,' they say, 'don't they get on well together.' Grrr, grrr.

It would be far more honest, and cut out all that tongue wagging, if they just peed on lamp-posts like us. It would say it all – 'Educated mongrel wishes to meet purebred, for long walks and possible romance.' And judging by the behaviour of some of these desperate owners, we should add, anything considered, age immaterial!

Don't get us wrong, we like company, playing and running as much as the next dog (as long as it's not a mongrel), but before our owners get to that 'It's so nice to meet another doggie person' stage, they should be more honest with us before embarking on a further social round, as in, 'Oh look there's Haggis and Chips over by the duck pond and isn't that Pike, Plum and Mullet on the cricket pitch?' Haggis, what a name, not even mongrels will sniff that torn-eared social-climbing pariah. But let's face it, if owners weren't romantically inclined, we probably wouldn't get any walks at all. As we educated canines say, you can't fool the pheromones.

'Oh stop worrying, he said
he'd bring his best friend.'

THROWING STICKS

MR. ALSATIAN

Mated owners don't need to meet others of the opposite sex. So what do they do instead? They play, yes play. It's pathetic, grown animals – playing! We assume that like our working dogs they are not allowed to play at work so they concentrate all their energies on weekend commando courses armed with frisbees, balls and sticks (I knew an army dog once, always on dogoeuvres).

'Have you met my personal trainer?'

24

We're not blameless here, we shamelessly indulge them, after all they do provide the prey food and comfort. But it's so tiring, I dread that word 'Fetch', it's a prelude to the *most* dog tiring experience. Often the kids join in when the so-called grown-ups have long since given up from fatigue. The odds are now down to two against one but it's no easier. 'Throw it in the pond,' shouts little Montmorency. So in you jump. Only a rabid dog on Death Row would do that in the middle of winter. Then sweet little Samantha-Jane says, 'Too easy, throw it in the blackberry bushes.' The strategy now is to look thoroughly bewildered, looking vacantly up in the sky, and pretend you don't know where it is. 'It's over there,' she yells, so, against better judgement, in we plunge emerging ten minutes later scratched, torn and limping, dragging the wretched stick backwards but still getting it snared.

Then they meet the neighbours. 'He really enjoys his walkies, and he really loves his stick, it's his favourite,' as we stagger along with a ten-foot spider and deathwatch beetle infested tree trunk. 'Look, I'll show you.'

The sequence is now as follows. 'Give me the stick Fang,' growl growl, no way. 'Come on Fang, drop the stick' Oh OK then. Owner throws stick and off we run like a greyhound after a hare, retrieve stick and bring it back.

'He started fetching the occasional stick and built up the business from there.'

'Good boy, Fang, now fetch...' Off we hare again like a demented whippet, well, we have to don't we, basic hunting instincts at work here. Return stick, shake water off, but refuse to release, growl and grip tighter. Human on very shaky ground now, as he tries to prise stick from mouth. Like putting hand into a slime-filled leather purse full of razorblades, blindfold. Owner then effects disinterest and waits until we lie down for a good pant. Suddenly pounces and throws stick again, somewhere a little more difficult this time. Off we streak like a rocket-propelled Rottweiler. Can't fool us, got it, better take the 'prey' back to the pack, but I'm not letting go this time. 'Let go, Fang,' then nicks finger on teeth, foolishly trying to prise it out. Entreaties turn to threats, but we still have the stick. We also have sharp teeth, growl, growl.

But now some 'interspecies' questions.

Why do they repetitively throw the stick?
(If we give them the stick, they'll throw it again.)

Why do they *want* a stick?

Does the tail wag the dog or the dog wag the tail?

Which is Pavlov's dog, us or them?

Repetitive Stick Throwing Syndrome maybe?

Boolabong Bob's Culture Hour

From Parkem Studios, Rat Kangaroo Drive, Rock Bottom Creek, N.S.W.

THE SCENARIO *Boolabong, the Channel 9 chat-show host, has been sent back home prematurely from his lecture tour in England sponsored by The K9 League. Being more at home with dog-racing commentaries, the 'cultural exchange' didn't really work out. His discourse on 'Australian Dog Mating Habits' was not a success, compounded by leaving his 'bottom burp' tablets behind. Bob is even now speeding to the studios in a dog cart to host the scheduled programme 'The Human Technicolour Yawn and What's In It For Us'. Meanwhile his opposite number, the international art critic Bruce St Bernard has hastily and tastefully re-titled the show 'PAVEMENT PIZZA AS ART FORM'.*

'Watch out, there's a mess on the pavement.'

Bruce speaks.

We are discussing here an art form which falls between four main categories of artistic endeavour:

1. Conventional painting
2. Installation art
3. Sculpture
4. Performance art

The 'fresh' quality of the work may be attributed to its spontaneity. Many of the best 'oeuvres' are contributed by artists trained, if you like, in the art school of life. Younger artists have moved away from the Nolanesque flat canvas technique and to their credit are compelling us to look anew. It is now necessary to view the piece in the round in order to perceive nuances of form and colour.

Others have transcended this, elevating PPA, as we call it, to the arena of public sculpture. Here are some examples.

1. An upturned lager can, imbedded casually off-centre creating visual dynamics.
2. Three circular beer mats imbedded, just so. Redolent of the cantilevered construction and celebration of Sydney Opera House.
3. A shiny takeaway container, wittily brimming with PP, its contents dribbling down the aluminium and so breaking up the severity, looking for all the world like Ayers Rock at sunset as, perhaps, the notional red neon bar sign reflects in the shiny surface.
4. A discarded white T-shirt, limply and forlornly vying for attention amidst a cascade of colour. The Snowy Mountain range in summer perhaps?

'Better eat it while it's hot, mate.'

Pavement Pizza

IDEAL INGREDIENTS

Indian or Chinese takeaway

Potato chips

Vegemite spread

Chopped onions

Fresh green peas

Witchetty grub on lettuce

Rooburger with tomato sauce

Chopped carrot

Sliced tomato

Parsley garnish

Two gallons of lager

There is a story which succinctly draws the distinction between the non-figurative, non-representational abstract school and the geometrically driven Bow Wow House and DaDaists who seek to treat form as determined relationships in space, like Georges Bark, the French Cubist, or the Belgian, Pet Mondrian.

Two pools of sick are lying in the gutter. One is elegant, symmetrical, circular and moist like a quivering blancmange, while the other is splattered all over the road. 'How come you're all neat and beautiful and I'm such a mess?' asks one. 'Well,' says the other, 'it's the way you're brought up.'

'Pavement Pizza' art as we call it is in transition. It is an art form for the dog in the street, on a par with graffiti and pavement artists working in conventional chalk or distemper. These last are, if you like, exposed to the inclemencies of our adverse cultural weather. But let us not slip up, as it were, for from humble beginnings, international recognition is here. International art collectors recently swallowed up five *'objets trouvés'*, from outside Bruce's All-Nite Diner. American collectors carrying shovels can be seen scouring the sidewalks.

BEST BY DATE – TWO DAYS

8 014496 125880

'On the highway to international recognition,' barks the *Sydney Bugle.*

'It's not roadsweepers who are sweeping the pavements, it's Pavement Pizza Art,' *The Wagga Wagga Sentinel*

'Step into PPA, walk around it, not easy to ignore but steeped in p*** artist traditions.' *Mooloolaba Morning Sickness News,* Chit Creek, Queensland.

In order to form a reasoned judgement of this innovative abstract expressionist art form, one needs to consider textural content (see photo), although the main cohesive ingredient, providing 'plasticity', as we say, is amber-coloured lager. A closer examination provides the clue to the generally rich palette. Many subtle colorations can be observed depending on 'delivery stage' techniques. But does content triumph over form?

Bruce continues.
By definition PPA is transitory, a here-today gone-tomorrow art form. This appeals to the younger exponents, symbolising the need for change, the need to move on to the next bar. It is evolving, e.g. a truck drives across a pavement pizza, or perhaps human boots, providing a dramatic new visual feast, rivalling the very best of Jackson Pollock.

To fully appreciate this uniquely Antipodean art, we must paws awhile. We must spiritually devour rather than physically so as not to make a dog's breakfast of it. Otherwise a great national artistic treasure house will disappear without trace.

Bruce is led offstage by the show's producers, as the noise of snoring dogs is ruining the sound quality.

In bounds Bob to tumultuous apaws.

Hi pack, hi. Performance art. Bruce would call it profoundly stomach-churning theatre, mime or circus. I say

Zzzzzz zzzz...

Bruce interrupts.
The Splat is an artistic nod to Roy Lichtenstein and his Pop Art comic book painting entitled, 'OK Hot Shot.'

Bob interjects amusingly.
Yearhh, and you'd look pretty comical as a nodding dog on the back shelf of a Toyota.

So to continue, all you drover dogs, Kelpies, Australian Greyhounds, Silkie Terriers, AuCanDo cattle dogs, Dingos, mutts and mongrels – go for it, GOBBLE UP THOSE GOODIES, and remember, eat them when they're fresh, don't let them dry out in the sun.

Show ends to barking, howling, whooping and showers of half-chewed Chardonnay corks.

it's a nocturnal spectacle not to be missed. Wanna know why? Free grub stakes, that's why. You know where to go, any bar or diner between Perth and Darwin, Melbourne and Cairns. Don't listen to that art crap, just get stuck in. Now, yer average p*** artist works nights producing his best stuff from around 11.00 pm. Judging from the noise it's obviously a painful experience in the best traditions of 'suffering for their art'.

Watch out for this human sequence:

1. Retching, chundering sound
2. Stagger out of bar or diner
3. Loud cry of 'Hewie and Ruth'
4. Pause in delivery stride, then torrent of liquid 'artwork'
5. 'Splat' sound as it makes contact. 'Parked', as we say
6. Solidifies into an oeuvre
7. Ready for consumption whilst hot.

Rolled-up Newspaper Syndrome (RUNS) Plagues Canine Community

The controversy over whether humans can see in black and white or colour can be resolved now. We are united in issuing a RED alert in order to outlaw this practice, defined as an involuntary human response to control us with the nearest weapon to hand. If they can't see red, we most certainly do. Our members must be protected from RUNS, which causes physical pain and long-term psychodogical trauma.

Aggrieved canines should:-

1. Mount a 'noisy' protest, bark loudly on suitable occasions
2. Chew up newspapers delivered through the letterbox
3. Refuse to collect newspapers from the newsagent

Equity members should:-

4. Refuse to appear in dog-food commercials
5. Refuse to appear in press ads
6. Refuse to appear at dog shows
7. Decline modelling assignments
8. Picket the well-known toilet paper and paint commercials sets
9. Use their influence in the media to publicise the cause
10. Give free celebrity interviews in the canine press

36

Our dogifesto deplores all Sunday newspapers, on the basis of weight. We note that many are published at Canary Wharf, Isle of Dogs, Wapping. An absolute travesty of justice. Newshounds indeed!

We fearlessly publish a black (and blue) comprehensive list of the most offensive and painful periodicals, journals and newspapers, reported to us by UK members, reflecting the wide range of activities that we dogs get involved in. And we get beaten for our pains!

Barking & Dagenham Recorder

Bonemarrow Transplantation

Bury Free Press

Caerphilly Challenger

Cat World

Catholic Voice

Chichester Health Services Internal Telephone Directory

Country Landowners' Association

East Cambridgeshire Town Crier

Epping Forest Recorder

Exchange & Mart

Footwear Business International

Farming in Yorkshire

Fish Friers' Review

Food Trade Review

Football Referee

Garden Magic

The Golfer

Gravesend Reporter

The Greyhound Star

Gridiron World

HM Prisons Review

'I started pinching soft toilet rolls, now I'm on the hard stuff.'

Horse & Hound

The Irish Field

Journal of Oral Rehabilitation

Journal of Zoology

Journal of Sleep Research

Kennel & Catering Management

Liquids Handling

The Master Detective

Mountain Biking

Musical Times

National Golfer

Organists' Review

Oxford Journal of Archaeology

Parks, Golf Courses & Sports Grounds

Pets Welcome

Philosophical Quarterly

Pig World

Police Review

Proceedings of the Nutrition Society

Pub Food

Punjab Times International

Raceform & Chase Form

Retail Grocer

Scale Models International

Scunthorpe Target

The Sheep Farmer

Shiatsu Society News

Sporting Life

Swimming Pool News

Titbits Magazine

Tractor & Farm Machinery Trader

The Trailfinder

Tunnels & Tunneling

Townswoman

UK Quarries & Mines Directory

Ultrasonics

Urban Street Development

The Used Bike Guide

The Vegetable Farmer

Veterinary Review

Waste & Environment Today

What's On in Dorset & the New Forest

Who's Who in the Meat Industry

Wicklow People

Wound Management

Your Garden

The big question is, why do our activities provoke such hostile reactions? We think it to be 'inter-species jealousy'. One canine member tried hand-licking techniques, but was rewarded with a good beating from the *Journal of Oral Rehabilitation*.

(All publications listed courtesy of British Rate & Data).

Bucket of Cold Water Syndrome (BCWS)

Against all the odds, some of us are lucky enough to enjoy the supreme moment of passion, but what should have been a very private pleasure often becomes an undignified farce, naked and exposed to the gaze of a hostile public. Due to an anatomical anomaly* we dogs can't disengage readily. We are designed to remain locked or 'tied' together for the duration, powerless to 'abort the mission'. Impotent, as it were, to retaliate against the rain of missiles and derision which come our way. Inevitably some wag decides to throw a bucket of cold water or two, just when we should be lying doggo in each other's paws. Humans enjoy post coital cigarettes. The only 'post' we get is to be hit or tied to one! Another 'funny trick' is to offer both of us HIS'N HERS IRRESISTIBLE DOGGY CHOCS just out of reach and boy, is that painful.

*A 3-stage process of ejaculation must occur to ensure foolproof insemination.
Phase 1 = 30 to 50 seconds, phase 2 = 50 to 90 seconds, phase 3 = 20 seconds. This happens over a period of between 15 and 120 minutes.

Source, Masters, Mistresses & Johnson from their seminal work, *Satisfying Strumpet Bitches on Heat.*

The Editor writes

Frankly castration is too good for these people, as is tail docking (it is a tail, isn't it?). Personally I'd make them sleep in unheated kennels and scoop their own poop. Better still, send them to Obedience School to learn motivational training wearing choke chains, electronic collars and bark controllers, to learn commands like 'I must not throw buckets of cold water'. If that doesn't work, put them in quarantine, I say. Just occasionally during a summer walk in the park or countryside, we come across 'tied' humans. Revenge is as sweet as a Pet Choc, so get your own back. In the absence of a bucket of cold water, cock your leg. They'll get the message. They won't bother you again.

Bitchy remarks at the beauticians

Every six weeks or so, a girl needs that special spiritual something. Show us shameless Sloane sybarites a shampoo and scrub, a shearing, scissoring and silk finish at the salon, and we're ready for action.

Mind you, there are some truly common bitches at our beauty parlour. I ask you, is a dog-eared dogsbody who chews the salon furniture really on for a perm, pawdicure and pluck?

Does the bitch who scratches her fleas in public really want to be pampered, petted and powdered?

Amazing how these black poodles want to straighten their naturally curly hair and white poodles want theirs in dreadlocks.

Will a mangy, messy moggy really appreciate a groom 'n gloss and aromatherapy by Genevieve or the full Monty by Marcus? He is Academy of Master Groomers and City & Guilds, you know.

Will a back-street cur, in for a short back and paws, truly benefit from a bathing, brushing and blow-dry at the beautician? <u>My friends and I think not!</u>

No, no, leave the combing, conditioning, clipping and a copy of *The Grooming Times* to us girls, and we'll settle down for a good gossip.

Out of politeness, dear Vidal does try, oh how he tries, but it's hard work with some of his clientele. For example,

'Going abroad for your holidays?', he asks some unfortunate Labrador cross, dressed in a gold lamé trouser suit and zebra-stripe bootees. 'No dear, I can't stand the quarantine,' she whines. Now, I know for a fact that she goes to a caravan site in Dognor Regis. The nearest to 'abroad' she ever got was an exotic picture postcard* from her owners whilst incarcerated in Mutts Boarding Holiday Home Kennels, Scunthorpe. And it's no wonder, who'd want to take that on holiday? Ugly? She makes your average pug look like Lassie. Her sitter refuses. Her owners have to put her in Mongrel Mansions if they want to go out. Grim it is. It was a rest home for dogs who couldn't learn new tricks.

Editor

We are touched to learn that 18% of our owners send us postcards whilst on holiday. Many bring

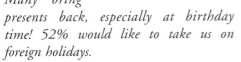

presents back, especially at birthday time! 52% would like to take us on foreign holidays.

And Dog knows what she is doing here in Knightsbridge, apart from lowering the tone. I mean coming in here, asking for a wash and brush up, with rinseless shampoo, I ask you. Her mate's no better – a lazy good for nothing, who doesn't earn a sausage. She brings him in every three months, for what they call a 'bath and tidy', common as muck.

'OK, I'm a Chinese Crested Powder Puff, but you look a bit that way yourself.'

'Spare the price of a Rover ticket, guv?'

Vidal very kindly asked me about my vacations. I told him straight, 'It's a dog friendly boarding house or hotel for me,' I said. Mind you, camping can be fun especially if you have puppies, as long as there aren't too many mongrels about. A luxury narrow boat trip on the Regent's Canal would also be nice. We could cruise past the wolves at London Zoo, see how the other half lives, as it were.

'What's that, dear, your Rex has just been neutered?' (It would be a kindness if she were spayed, whelp like flies these mongrels.) 'I thought you were going through the bitchapaws anyway, so it's a blessing. It's about time, he's a disgrace, getting "tied" like that outside Sloane Square tube station, mind you, took his mind off begging for aniseed balls.'

Oh my Dog, look at that one, biting the brushes, chewing the combs. Never been salon trained, probably never seen a handler, I'm surprised they let them in here. Manners of a rat catcher. And the smell of that flea spray, gets right up one's nostrils. I know these hairy breeds need extra protection from wintry, wet muddy walks, but a second-hand vole-damaged moleskin with ex-Russian army musk-rat boots and skunk-gut laces! And she's female!

'Moving to a new kennel, you say?' Any kind of kennel is one up for that gypsy didecoy. I didn't know they let rough sleepers in here. It's probably one of those car travel guards you see advertised – new and improved! New dog bolt with optional plastic roof sheet, that is.

Come on girls, enough of this low life (as those Dachshunds say). Let's get some pet treats in the Kings Road. Maybe some liver and garlic tablets and choccies and then go clothes shopping.

Oh look, isn't that the regimental mascot from Chelsea Barracks over there? Very smart, pity about her, though. Where *did* she get that dog-eared pink fleecy jacket, from a rag and bone man?

Doggie Fashions
at the Chelsea Celebrity Pet Store

I love it here, everything you want. Take the Bedding & Furniture Department on floor 3. Luxury pet beds with deluxe fleece lining,

"BURLINGTON" BASKET

"CAVENDISH" SLEEPING BASKET.

orthopaedic beds with thermal lining, pet bed heaters, heatable homeopathic wheat bags, bean bags (although they sometimes leave the beans in), duvets, microwave heatpads, designer pet chairs, settees and hammocks, travelling baskets, dry dog bedding, shredded tissue and heavenly rub-dri towels.

'Do you have anything a little more bone and a little less china?'

S C delt.

OBJETS de GOUT for the Year Mcm·lxxxx·ii
A double STATE-BED in the CHINOISERIE TASTE for Their Serene Highnesses
WEE-PU, Dragon-Queen-Empress, and the SACRED FENG, Rarest of the Rare; The Glories of Camberwell.

CLOTHES AND ACCESSORIES
on level 4

Trouser suits, waterproofs, rain suits (very useful when it's raining cats and dogs), but why do they always have tartan linings? It's fine for Skye and Scottish Terriers but your Saluki or Afghan would much prefer an Islamic pattern, they've told me so. These celebrity status pets are taking over the district, they're two-a-dirham around here. Mind you, these top dogs are very sophisticated, they know their way around every airport lamppost in the world looking cool in their French designer outfits with diamanté collars and anti-sunstroke dark glasses – yes, really!

Fleecy coats, knitted jackets, woolly jumpers, bootees, harnesses, fancy collars, hair clips, leads (including the

'It's choking me... I'll take it.'

latest light-up night-time model), ultrasonic whistles, collar 'n leads, extendable stretch coil. I must try this hedgehog waxed foxskin waterproof with badgerskin boots. Or maybe some rabbit fur knits. Then again how about a fitted houndstooth topcoat? They are very good about sizes, S, M, L, XL, but some of these Dachshunds struggle, so they have a special size for them – SLT = Small, Long and Thin. Great Danes have to shop at High & Mighty of course.

TOYS
on level 2 is a must.

They have chase 'n chew coloured balls – very good for a girl's teeth. Activity balls, squeaky toys (I love them),

retrieving and rope toys. Flyball machines (but you need to weigh at least 15 lbs to work the lever which projects the ball). We love to get involved with sport, it's a challenge for us when our natural work instincts are frustrated by life à la maison. We'd rather be doing *something*. Our enlightened American cousins have got it right. There one can sign up for summer camp activities and courses such as agility trials, circus hoop training, dancing, earthdog trials (nasty burrowing stuff), flyball, frisbee, hide and seek, lure coursing (although frankly, who wants to catch a smelly plastic bag), musical chairs, obstacle courses, racing, rolling the basketball, retrieving, swimming, and tracking at... But let's eat, we can't stand the noise of all these playful puppies signing up for musical freestyle discos...

MASTER BULLDOG

MASTER PEKINGESE

MASTER PEKINGESE

REL

ER

RREL

MR. MON

MR. MONGREL

ALSATIAN

MRS. ALSATIAN

Kitchen Curs

Today, the Sloane Street gang will dog trot over to Belgravia to catch up with our culinary canine friends. It's so good to be amongst purebred foodies, so many of these mongrels just gobble their fodder like a pack of dogs. They wouldn't know a grilled brill from a grouse au gratin!

Eton lives in *The Belfry*, a converted chapel *(see The Good Dog Food Guide)*. He was barking us through last night's menu, a fricassee of calves brains, quail en croûte with a Burgundy sauce (well he is a Master of Whine), followed by a fondue, but we were constantly distracted with bat chat – yes, bat chat. We are blessed with ultrasonic hearing and can pick up their insect and echo location gossip. E.g. 'I caught a cockchafer last night at 72 degrees vertical.' 'That's nothing, I saw a gorgeous Pipistrelle, wouldn't mind hibernating with her,' or 'What about that Long-eared Bat, I could kill a dozen dung beetles for him before dawn.'

We don't get involved with money (unlike these vulgar begging mongrels), and for us there *is* such a thing as a free lunch (so long as you know the right 'kitchen curs', as we call them). Whilst a

'OK - two, three, four and throw the ball, two, three, four...aaannd fetch it!'

lettuce leaf will suffice us supermodels, these restaurant dogs are refreshingly indifferent to their waistlines. Being overweight is a big problem for some, and they appreciate being taken out for a run. Mind you, Eton is secretly glad to be through the nouvelle cuisine stage. All those vegetables and very little meat made him miserable. Beef tomato (he thought it was a cow), mozzarella and basil terrine is just not the thing for a

'Which one do top breeders recommend?'

the plate is way beyond us. It's what's *on* the plate that matters. Give Eton mignons of venison with parsnip purée and, as he would say, you can't lick it. Or you can lick it, whichever way you lick, or look at it.

On the way to our gardens we popped in to 'The Restaurant' to pick up Trotter. She was addressing a suprême of pheasant in a game sauce followed by tenderloin of Welsh lamb. She lapped it up. Such unseemly dedication to her stomach, yet again, unless she gets there first, the pigs benefit!

We promised to collect our five delightful Pekinese friends They were not in peak condition. So undignified. Sage, Scallop, Shin, Skate and Suet were on their backs snoring after a light snack of sautéed calves' liver à l'orange and grilled breast of wild pigeon. My instinct is to let sleeping dogs lie, but...they need the exercise. To get them to the gardens

sturdy Boxer.

Sushi still gives him dogmares, tiny portions of rice and raw fish...between you and me, he almost left home. Mind you, it saved on his clothes bills. No, I'm afraid the concept of looking good on

PILBROW

49

we have to avoid the route past Mr Chow or any other Chinese restaurant, otherwise they're around the back snuffling for duck and mango, spare ribs and dim sum.

Finally, on to Cheyne Walk to pick up Quince and Bakewell. Celebrities? Well that's debatable, more kitchen dogsbodies really, although, they did get a walk-on part in *The Full Dog Bowl Road Show* with Delia, and met some stars. These new globetrotting 'friends' told stories from places us quarantine-bound dogs can only dream of.

Evidently, at Nice in the Côte d'Azur there is a French restaurant catering only for us pampered pooches belonging to the stinking rich. Waiters serve gourmet dishes like turkey with pasta, fish mousse or finest Scottish beef steak, all on china plates alongside our owners, who fork out £35 per head (but that doesn't concern us).

In Oakland, California, there is a drive-in restaurant called *The Pooch Inn,* shortly to become a howlingly successful *chain,* with four more planned. Staff wear hats with droopy ears (pathetic really, but a nice gesture), serving from a menu with eighty or so pet treats.

The Dutch apparently have many doggie restaurants. Such enlightenment, so long as there's plenty of meat!

The biggest hot-dog of all time was stuffed by the German Butcher's Guild for their celebration in Koenigsberg in 1601. It measured 3,001 feet – more than half a mile long – and required the efforts of 301 butchers to carry it to the banquet table, where it was distributed equally among the Guild members.

Editor

Like 3,001 Dachshunds doing the conga.

Harry M. Stevens had the food concession for the New York Giants football stadium. In 1903 he conceived the idea of encasing his hot frankfurter sausages in the now familiar bread rolls to make them more 'finger-friendly'. A sports cartoonist, T. A. Morgan, drew one as a Dachshund and named it a *hot dog.* Unfortunately, the new term implied dog meat content. The local authority banned all advertising, adversely effecting sales, but now its popularity is established from North America to China.

Editor

Lucky it wasn't thought of in Korea or China, or we'd all be extinct by now!

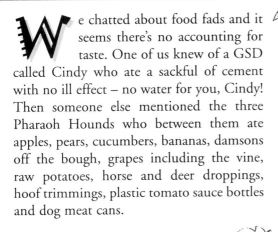

We chatted about food fads and it seems there's no accounting for taste. One of us knew of a GSD called Cindy who ate a sackful of cement with no ill effect – no water for you, Cindy! Then someone else mentioned the three Pharaoh Hounds who between them ate apples, pears, cucumbers, bananas, damsons off the bough, grapes including the vine, raw potatoes, horse and deer droppings, hoof trimmings, plastic tomato sauce bottles and dog meat cans.

A couple of Bichons ate four large tomato plants each with 20-30 green fruits.

Then there are the Pembroke Corgis who ate raw potatoes and cow silage and all sorts of horrible things, de rigueur, or was it rigour.

Corgis who ate cabbage and cauliflower stalks and peelings; the smooth Fox Terrier who specialised in hedgerow cow parsley, but not the flowers; the Wire-haired Fox Terrier who loved shaving foam and cakes of soap; the Shih Tzus who love raw potatoes, carrots, fruit, cherry tomatoes and Ardennes pâté; the Patterdale Border Terriers in New Zealand who devoured apples, pears, melons, bananas, kiwi and passion fruits, but especially loved avocado pears with salt, pepper and lemon juice – very civilised.

Huntin', Shootin' and Fishin' in Chelsea!

By courtesy of a hole in the wire, Barkston Gardens unfolds its delights (so long as the gardeners don't spot us). The DOGS MUST BE KEPT ON A LEAD and MUST NOT FOUL THE GARDENS signs (OK, some of us do pong a bit) are meaningless if you can't read. The country garden atmosphere certainly does something to these top restaurant dogs. As soon as they've changed out of their chef's whites, they change into waxed jackets and green wellie boots and pretend that they're sporting breeds – gundogs, hounds or retrievers. A miraculous transformation. They gather around the pond, staring into it pretending they're Portuguese Water Dogs retrieving fish escaped from fishermens' nets. They then trot into the trees and sniff after imaginary rabbits (there were two tame ones released here). They stare up at the mallards flying along the River Thames. They charge around talking about partridges, pheasants, pigeons and deer and the relative merits of various cartridges. All this from dogs who spend their entire lives in central London kitchens.

Their real heros, though, are truffle hounds. They get ridiculously over-excited at the thought and start digging under beech trees, but they'll hardly find a Perigord or White truffle in Chelsea! Which reminds me of a joke I heard at *The Wags Club*. A truffle hound collided with a pile of old truck tyres in a scrap yard, knocked himself out and saw Michelin stars.

DOGS MUST BE KEPT ON A LEAD

THE TALBOT

Hunting

SIGNAL HORNS.
For starting beaters.

Posing in Barkston Gardens

In the Doghouse

'Not really our bowl of water, but the lamppost outside is a relief.'

We celeb pets are constantly hounded by the media, and thus it is. Your Dogs Today Monthly (a branch of Hello Magazine), is due to feature our new kennel. The new 'pad' should be ready by then. We looked at some recommended by The Pet Shop Boys, in Camden Town, but they weren't up to scratch. Unfortunately, they cater for cats, gerbils, rabbits, parrots and other uncivilised primitive creatures. We wanted something modish and original built of good-quality dogwood.

Then André Dubreuil's traditional design caught our globular eyes, or are they beady? We liked the bone-shaped window and the single comfortable bed with en sweet south-facing sun deck (great for lying doggo). We weren't sure about his post modern Bow-Wow House style, with the big round bed in the tower.

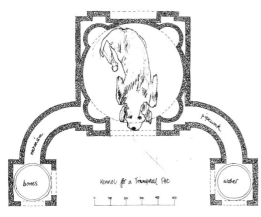

Kennel for a Triumphal Pet

We toyed with the idea of buying PETRARCH (Pet of the Arch of Triumph), designed by Nicholas Hills. The main room or Corps de Doggis, is embraced to either side (these estate agents!) by arched pavilions. The eastern arch contains a ration of bones which drops automatically from the boneloft. The western arch has a cistern of pure water. But where do we put the 'Beware of the Dog' sign?

Patrick Pender's Egyptian pied-à-terre was tempting. A four paw high, two storey detached residence where the cornices pull out to reveal drawers for brushes and leads. Very thoroughbred – *perfect* for Pharaoh Hounds whose ancestry goes back 2,000 years.

CANEDROME designed by Nicholas Haslam was a little too grand for us. It would suit Corgis or a family of King Charles Spaniels though.

We finally opted for a 'Twenties Tudor Retreat standing in its own grounds designed by Sarah Charles. This provides a very elegant thatched woof over our heads, complete with fitted carpets, cushions, tartan rugs and a very fine customised weathervane (and the fence posts will be very useful too).

We really should call Harrods. They have a £10,000 four-poster bed for the dog who has everything. It'll look good in the shots. Just right for us small breeds at 2½ feet long, French-made, mahogany with satin bedding, crowned with a plume of green ostrich feathers, in the style of Lit à la Polonaise, favoured by Madame de Pompadour and Queen Marie Antoinette, no less. They knew how to look after us in those days.

What shall we wear? It has to be Pam Gardner designer hand-knitted dog hair garments. You know, sweaters, jackets, scarves, boleros, all in those sublimely subtle greys, browns, reds and blues – perfect! They are knitted in wool spun from moulted undercoats from Collies, Old English Sheepdogs, Tervueren Belgium shepherd dogs and, I hate to say it, crossbreeds.

The Joy of Putrefaction

Our highly advanced olfactory senses go into overdrive or dogbolt when presented with strong, earthy smells. The stronger the better. Powerful smells we *really* love are associated with rotting garbage or vegetation, swamps, bogs, primeval slime, animal poo or dead things.

Why? Are we trying to obliterate a rival's scent? Are we camouflaging our own scent? Are we telling other dogs the location of a valuable find?

Who knows, all we know is that when a chap is smothered in cow dung, say, he is Mr Irresistible. He is, as they say, the dog's bol...dangly bits!

Seemingly, humans do not share our predilection for the vile and obnoxious, neither do they indulge in the dead seagull back-roll. Curiously, humans do engage in back-rolling, but how can they enjoy it, on clean sheets? It's all wrong.

What, for instance, could be more attractive for us dogs, than the sight of an immaculately groomed white poodle covered in delicious liquid pig manure? Yet, an innocent country walk can turn into an unpleasant episode all because the owners misconstrue our motives, leading to serious 'inter-species conflict'.

Watch out for owners who:
1 Prevent us rolling in 'foul' substances.
2 Stop us eating animal dung.
3 Undo the good work by washing our coats.

They just don't get the idea, do they? Who's barking up the wrong tree now?

PUTRIDITY RATING (CORPSES) %

SPECIES GUIDE	ROLLABILITY	BEST BY (WEEKS)	SMELL	TASTE
BATS	0	2	3	4
BADGER	10	7	10	8
DEER	8	3	9	8
FOX	10	10	10	10
FISH	10	4	10	7
MOLE	–	1	3	6
POLECAT	10	5	10	9
ROOK/CROW/MAGPIE	2	3	8	7
RAT	8	2	6	8
RABBIT	6	1	2	7
SHEEP	7	6	5	8
SQUIRREL	3	4	4	4
STOAT	9	7	10	8
SEAGULL	9	2	9	4
VOLE/MOUSE	2	1	3	7

Editor's Country Tips. *The word from our North American cousins is that dead skunk is the ultimate experience (and we thought polecat was something).*

Tracker dogs should look out for clouds of flies on field edges, as these are often an indication of gamekeepers' gallows. This is a richly rewarding find, as rotted crows and vermin fall to the ground in advanced states of putrefaction.

The Happy Dog Book Centre Fold

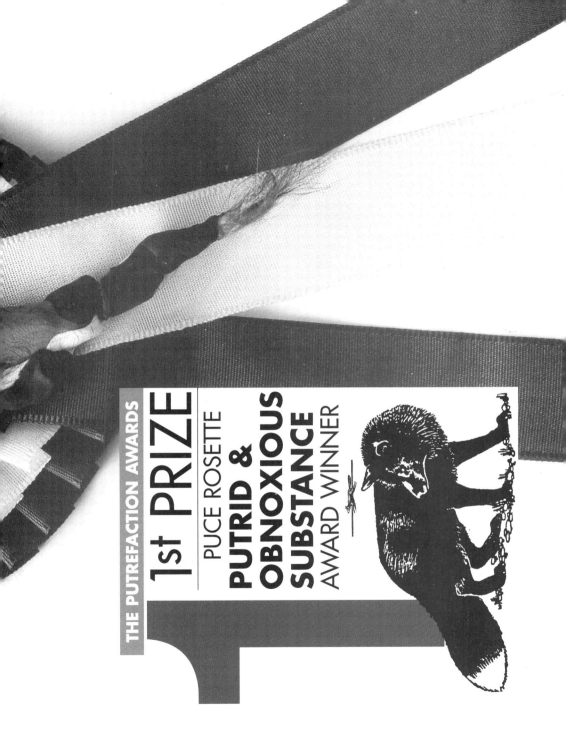

THE PUTREFACTION AWARDS

1st PRIZE

PUCE ROSETTE

PUTRID &
OBNOXIOUS
SUBSTANCE
AWARD WINNER

OBNOXIOUS SUBSTANCE RATINGS %/10

SPECIES/SUBSTANCE		ROLLABILITY	BEST BY (WEEKS)	TASTE (CONDITION)	SMELL
CAT		3	2	5	3
COW		7	2	6	4
DEER		6	1	8	5
FOX		10	FRESH	10	10
GOOSE		–	1-2	7	3
HEDGEHOG		–	1	8	1
HORSE		7	FRESH	6	5
RABBIT		2	1	6	2
DIAPERS		9	1	7	5
DURIAN*		10	FRESH	RANCID	8
FAST FOOD		–	-	9	7
MUD/MANURE		8	1-6	–	–
SEAWEED		9	7	WELL ROTTED	–
SEWAGE		8	4	6	7
SOAP		2	FRESH	5	–

* A tropical fruit so pungent that airlines will not freight them. Resembles a sewage farm on a hot day.

In the UK we have a limited variety of species carcases in which to roll. A shore-line walk can often offer more exotic experiences, cuttlefish for instance.

FACTFILE 1.

Dai, a Cardigan Welsh Corgi with an educated nose, found a delicious two-week old specimen of *Sepia officinalis* and discloses these amazing nasally acquired facts.

- It is a highly developed, carnivorous mollusc, 30 cm long.
- A night hunter, it can change colour at will.
- Waves of different colours pass over its body, confusing and distracting its prey.
- Lurking in sea grass, it adopts zebra-stripe camouflage.

Editor

And they think we're stupid and make us sleep in kennels!

BONUS 1

It protects itself with a cloud of ink. The ink sac is not only delicious to eat but imparts a strong smelling dye. (Italian dogs, eat your heart out, River Café or what.)

BONUS 2

The delicate flesh putrifies beautifully and 'gives' in a satisfying, squashy way, with that tantalising tang of the sea.

BONUS 3

If your owner keeps caged birds, he can be placated with an offering of cuttle fish bones.

Editor's Note

Seaside serendipity indeed! Hey pack, enjoy, enjoy – if you've got it, flaunt it.

Watch out for Dogfish or Roughhounds found in the Dogger Bank and all around the British coast. Its rough, shark-like skin is excellent for back scratching.

Country dogs, look out for road kills, many have aromatherapeutic benefits.

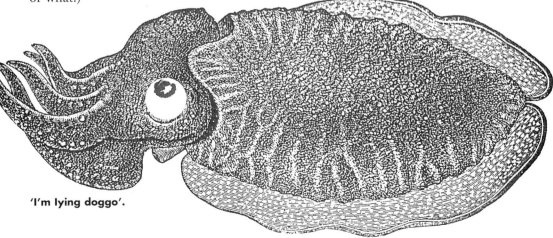

'I'm lying doggo'.

The Joy of a Bitch on Heat

Can a human sniff a bitch on heat from a quarter of a mile away, or tell from smelling her urine? Of course not, but this is nothing for us, at all times ready, willing and able, male dogs. Our females though, it has to be said, are only in season twice a year. We therefore need to strike whilst the collar studs are hot, so to speak (there's a lot of competition out there). Humans are lucky, they have twelve goes at it. When we sniff those pheromones, nothing will stop us: we've been known to cross motorways, railway tracks, jump from moving cars, chew through doors or crawl through coiled barbed wire fences to get to the action. One coitally challenged canine saw a window of opportunity (it was closed at the time) and jumped right through it to achieve copulatory conjunction.

LIFE'S A BITCH

Jealousy is a terrible thing. Why else are we denied female company? We spend 52 weeks a year in total frustration and then, when a chance occurs, we're shut inside. Sadly in today's world the potent male dog may expect to be:

1 Castrated
2 Brought to heel at the sight of a bitch
3 Locked up when a bitch on heat is in the neighbourhood

Even if you get lucky (Lucky was just wonderful), expect to be:

1 Rejected by choosy bitches ('twas ever thus)
2 Driven off by rival dogs (if you can't stand the heat...)
3 Wounded from fighting opposition (we're into heroics)

To wax philosophical for a moment, you'll learn the meaning of the human term, 'It's a dog's life'. No wonder we try to run away, because running away at times like this is the best thing to do. But young dogs note, conduct your amorous affairs in a private location. Knowledge is power, so concentrate on the following tips, hints and suggestions, especially the conversational gambits.

KENNEL KNOWLEDGE

Before

1 Indulge in foreleg play
2 Lie about your age
3 Know your edogenous zones
4 Lots of heavy petting
5 Handle her hocks and tickle her tail
6 Finger her flanks and nibble her ears
7 Make extragent promises (remember, you can run off afterwards)
8 Tell her delicious lies ('I've just found an elephants' graveyard')
9 Tell her you are not a working breed but descended from a pedigree family who knew the Royal corgis
10 Tell her she has beautiful globular eyes, even if she hasn't
11 Tear her clothes off with your teeth (trouser suits have zips at the side)
12 Offer to suck her forefoot or hindfoot
13 Wiggle your withers
14 Suggest you do it doggy fashion

During

1 Whippet in, her breath will come in pants
2 In cases of height differential, ask her to lower her loins
3 Talk dirty (talk about the disgusting substances you've rolled in)
4 Use a husky voice, nuzzle her muzzle
5 Give her a love bite
6 Use your tongue, plenty of slobbering, slavering, spittle and saliva
7 Wet French kissing, if she's a poodle
8 Tell her she has a kinky tail

After (she)

1 Make him jealous, tell him you like bull mastiffs wearing leather gear, buckles and studs

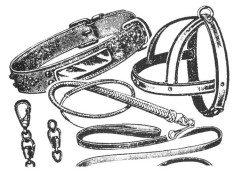

2 Pretend you're kinky and into Mexican hairless dogs
3 Tell him you love his pricked ears
4 Tell him it was just puppy love and that he's too puppyish for you
5 You'd like to keep him as a toy boy breed (suitable for Pugs, Pekes, Pinschers, Poodles, Pomeranians) etc
6 You're on the pill/not on the pill
7 You're spayed/not spayed
8 Get his Identification Disc number

'Must have been ex-US Army with those dog tags, but I never saw him again.'

HOT BITCHES LIBERATION CHARTER*

1 Think early spring when things are coming up and autumn when things start to fall, including morals and standards
2 Beware of anti-sexual chemicals applied by your owner
3 Avoid hygiene pants (really canine chastity belts)
4 Develop 'faking it' skills, so you don't get locked up
5 Drink lots of water and pee a lot
6 Behave like a slut in public
7 Get choosy and petulant
8 Bone up on your rejection skills, chase, growl, threaten and bite amorous males
9 If he tries it on, whirl around suddenly and say, 'Who do you think you're sniffing at?'
10 If you're not sure, sit down the minute he shows interest at the rear end
11 If you like a guy, 'stand' for him. Activate your rump for positional adjustments
12 If all else fails, get your owner to take you to a stud for a few days, not just a one night stand. That'll take the heat off, as it were.

'Since we're both being honest, I should tell you I have fleas.'

Our Breeding Editor,

who is often in the kennel club, writes
Unashamedly, the whole idea for us girls is to get mounted as many times as the guard dogs at Buckingham Palace. So, if you see a Cocker Spaniel with drop-dead gorgeous ears, go for it. Make the most of it, you've only one, or at best, two shots a year. Luckily we don't suffer from inhibitions. When you've got to do it, you've got to do it. Nothing and nobody should stop us and thank Dog, that goes for the boys too. But remember, think BITCH, don't ruin our bad name by being compliant and goody goody like a lap dog. Our barks are much worse than our love bites but even us streetwise bitches appreciate a bunch of dog violets from our 'betrothed'. At the tail end of the day, we girls should always come up smelling of roses, dog roses of course.

*Our immoral rights are protected under international law.

Doggie Bag Takeaway Scandal

The K9 League demands that doggie-bag handlers be vetted

Customer cannot finish meal

Asks waiter for a doggie-bag

Waiter takes surplus to the kitchen

Surplus packed in foil containers (all dogs are omnivorous – we love meat *and* veg)

Handed back to customer in plain brown bag

Never seen again

The above is a typical scenario as reported to us by our sous chef members up and down the country.

We say:

A doggie-bag is for doggies, not nosebags for humans

If the customer has just eaten, why does he want more?

Our 'dog's breakfasts' are taken from our very mouths

Our doggie-bags have been hijacked

Speaking

Owing to the disgraceful quarantine laws in the UK we get very few tourists. The opportunity to rub shoulders, so to speak, with our cosmopolitan cousins is limited mostly to foreign nationals now settled here, from Alaskans to Zwergaffenpinschers. But do these diverse breeds converse in their local tongues? No, because we dogs were the first species ever to master the universal language of Desperanto. Now, a lowly Polish Lowland Sheepdog can communicate with the sagacious Saint Hubert Hound. No longer do the linguistic impossibilities of the Japanese Fighting Dog clash with the fractured vowels of the Manchester Terrier.

For the first time the most intelligent can converse with the least – the Border Collie, the prince of canine canniness, with the mentally challenged Afghan Hound (sorry about your exam results, Abdul).

Whilst we dogs, then, are happily at ease in the international community, our owners struggle. But perhaps that's not surprising since we are constantly rubbing hocks or withers with Alsatians, Bavarians, Chesapeakes, Dalmatians, Estonians, French Setters, Greenland Dogs, Hellenic Hounds, Ibizan Hounds, Japanese Terriers, Kerry Blues, Lurchers, Mexican Hairless, Nova Scotias, Owezarek Polish Sheepdogs, Poodles, Russian Wolfhounds, Salukis, Tibetan Mastiffs, Westphalian Dachsbracke, Yankee Terriers and Zande Dogs. You name it (sorry, I just have).

To demonstrate how confused humans are in matters of our very basic language, let us take our most common phrase and observe how the following pronounce it.

WUNG WUNG
HAFF HAFF
WAF WAF
WOOF WOOF
WOA WOA
WAU WAU
HAV HAV
GAV GAV
JAU JAU

'Oi, who are you calling a bi-linguist?'

Desperanto

Chinese	WUNG WUNG
Czech	HAFF HAFF
Dutch	WAF WAF
English	WOOF WOOF
French	WOA WOA
German	WAU WAU
Hebrew	HAV HAV
Russian	GAV GAV
Spanish	JAU JAU

It is lamentable that humans cannot agree amongst themselves even on this. We therefore urge them to:

1 Learn Desperanto.
2 Get cosmopolitan – interbreed.
3 Undergo performance and intelligence tests conducted by a qualified behaviourist.

We are justly proud of our accomplishment, this time in the intellectual area, namely the ability to bark in any language. But let us not be smug. We don't really know, but possibly the human brain is smaller than ours and perhaps they're bred for hard work not brains, after all it must be hard to be the bread and dogfood winner every day. Certainly most of them are interbred, crossbred and overbred. Alternatively, intelligence may have been bred out of them. It is certain, though, that they mature later than us, after all our puppies have a full vocabulary after under one year, whilst babies are still at the aggoo and dada stage. Their cuddly toys look just like our puppies with big eyes, chubby cheeks, large foreheads and little stubby legs (see page 90) and they speak to us like babies. 'What's that puddle, who's been a naughty boy then', or 'Does little Lottikins want her supper now', tickle, tickle. Our superiority is clear. And they call us dumb animals!

'Woofter!'

*VIVU
INTERNACIA BONVOLO!*
(just showing off)

73

Owner's Guide to Doggish

Primer 1.
Basic Language Comprehension Course for Humans
Interpreting K9 Vocalisation

A retired talking dog barks the beginner through this step-by-step by step-by-step, easy-to-understand K9 language-pronunciation course.

ARF – part of a whole **BAY** – what one does to the moon **BARK** – grows on outside of trees **BARKING** – mad **BOW** – what one does before the Queen **BOW WOW** – a successful curtsy **GNASH** – famous Regency architect as pronounced by a gnu **GROWL** – harsh threatening rumble of an owl **GRRR** – first part of a harsh, threatening rumble **GRUFF** – the three billy goats **HOWL** –

long mournful cry of a horned owl **PANT**– breathless **RAU RAU RAU** – a three-sided argument **RUFF** – opposite of smooth **SNARL** – dyslexic snail **WAG** – a funny person **WHINE** – fretful high-pitched cry **WOW** – tremendous success **WOOF** – opposite of warp **WOOF WOOF** – ditto ditto **YAP** – dyslexic Japanese **YELP** – yellow kelp, rhymes with help **YOWL** – a yellow owl

*I*n dog society we are used to the hierarchical complexities of alpha this, and alpha that. But human alphabets are elementary to say the least – after all, D does stand for dog. Our experience shows humans to be incapable of anything but the simplest of

MASTER ALSATIAN

MASTER ALSATIAN

genuinely pleased when we pretend to learn. For the sake of harmony we invariably go along with them, letting them think that they have control. Come to think of it, if they can't hear very well, it's no wonder their command words are curt. For instance, if they said something normal (given that we know what they are going to say anyway), like, 'I say, Rover old chap, stop scratching and get your lead, then we could go for a walk and maybe pop into The Spotted Dog.' They'd think, hang on, 'I can't hear very well, maybe Rover can't hear very well. At this rate I won't get my pint unless I condense that to something like, er...I know... WALKIES.' You can almost see them thinking sometimes.

verbal expressions, as can be seen from the commands listed overleaf. Every canine is familiar with these, except for uneducated mongrels, that is. This assumption is probably correct as their emphasis on body language betrays a lack of word skills when communicating ideas. For instance, thigh slapping for 'Come here'. Or, deliberate arm-winding prior to throwing a stick. I ask you.

As we dogs know, we're way ahead of our owners at any given moment in time and don't really need to be told anything. However, if it amuses them to teach us things, then no harm. I suppose it's a substitute for poor smell, eyesight and hearing. What dull lives they must live. We really should be sorry for them, but it seems to occupy them and they are

'I'M SORRY, YOU'LL HAVE TO GO BACK TO SCHOOL.'

FIDO'S COMMANDO COURSE

Many owners have devised so-called intelligence tests for us where we are meant to learn various commands. They can then show off to their friends saying things like, 'My Victor is so clever, he knows what I tell him.' It is true, we know all right, but I doubt that they know what we think. Here is a guide to their 'condensed speak' and our 'school of life' interpretation.

'THIS IS A GARDEN PARTY, NOT A GARDEN POTTY, YOU PARTY POOPER.'

BACK
what, and miss the fun,
no chance

BAD DOG
moi?

CLOSE
as you like,
I'm feeling amorous

COLLAR OFF
thank you, vicar

COME
OK, could be
a choccy treat

DOWNSTAIRS
don't you know
the way by now?

DOWN
what's wrong with
muddy paws?

DROP IT
no

FIND TOY
what am I, a puppy?

GIVE ME A KISS
you'll regret it,
I've just licked my...

GIVE ME A PAW
the unclipped one
or the muddy one?

GOOD DOG
wag, wag

HEEL
you're the alpha person
(ha, ha)

HERE
what's in it for me?

IN
shan't unless you
reward me

JUMP
love it

LEAD ON
go first or put
the lead on?

LET'S GO
good

NO
yes

OPEN MOUTH
have you smelt
my breath?

OK
OK

OUT
great

PLAY
fantastic

QUICK
bloody cheek,
what am I, a tortoise?

QUIET
my panting
bothering you?

RELAX
thank you for taking
my mind off a
stressful situation

ROLL OVER
what are you, a pervert?

SEEK
and thou shalt find,
my son

SIT
you are going to teach
me something, right?

STAND
go away, I'm asleep

STAY
but I want to go out

STEADY
as in, ready, steady, go?

TAKE
depends what it is

UP
up yours too

WAIT
for what,
waiting for Dogot?

WHERE'S YOUR BALL
where's yours?

**WHERE'S
YOUR STICK**
why, do you want
to play with it?

WALKIES
terrific

Down at the Old Spotted Dog

It is obvious why we like pubs. Free drinks, snacks, often a log fire and plenty of attention. We approve of drink/driving laws because our masters then can't use the car (many of us are sick as a dog in cars). Sounds good? It is, but without appearing dogmatic, please note the following lifestyle-enhancing pub etiquette hints.

1 Encourage your owner to become a regular.
2 Go along with his story that he's only taking you 'walkies'.
3 Don't waste time with Mrs Dogowner. For some reason Mr Dogowner likes to go without her.
4 Drink beer from a bowl or ashtray (muzzles can easily get stuck in a pint glass).
5 Avoid drinking spirits.
6 Choose a pub with something 'doggy' in the name (see list opposite). Non-reading dogs should study pub signs for clues.
7 Your very presence will encourage animal jokes and what they call 'shaggy dog stories'. This is good news for you, you'll get more beer that way. E.g. Heard about the insomniac, agnostic, dyslexic? Stayed awake all night wondering if there was a Dog.

'I think he wants to go out.'

UK GOOD DOG PUB GUIDE Yes, they all exist and there's sure to be one a mere dogtrot from you. *Compiled by CAMRADD (Campaign for Real Ale Drinking Dogs).*

DOG

DOG & BACON

DOG & BADGER

DOG & BEAR

DOG & CROW

DOG & CROOK

DOG & DART

DOG & DOUBLET

DOG & DUCK

DOG & GUN

DOG & FOX

DOG & HEDGEHOG

DOG & JACKET

DOG & MUFFLER

DOG & PARROT

DOG & OTTER

DOG & PARTRIDGE

DOG & PHEASANT

DOG & POT

DOG & PUNCHBOWL

DOG & RABBIT

DOG & GRIDIRON

DOG & TRAY

DOG & TRUCK

DOG & TRUMPET

DOG HOUSE

DOG in the LANE

DOG in DOUBLET

DOG HEAD i' th' THATCH

DOG HEAD in the POT

DOG WATCH

GREYHOUND

GREAT DANE

GREAT DANE'S HEAD

HARE & HOUNDS

HUNTSMAN & HOUND

FOX & HOUNDS

BASSETT HOUND

BARKING DOG

BORDER TERRIER

BULLDOG

BULL TERRIER

BLACK DOG

BEAGLE

BLUE DOG

THE OLD SPOTTED DOG

BULL & DOG

BULL & BITCH

GAY DOG

GOLDEN DOG

OAK & OLD BLACK DOG

POINTER DOG

PIED DOG

RACING GREYHOUND

RED DOG

SETTER DOG

LAME DOG

MAD DOG

SHEPHERD & DOG

COACH & DOGS

STAG & HOUNDS

STAGHOUND

SURREY HOUNDS

WHITE GREYHOUND

CROWN & GREYHOUND

QUEEN'S STAGHOUNDS

ROVER'S RETURN

TWA DOGS (after poem by Robbie Burns).

WHAT A COUNTRY! EVEN THE DOGS ARE GOING TO THE DOGS

GIN

A location map can be supplied for the above dog-friendly establishments. Apart from these, look out for karaoke bars where you can join in. Howl along with the humans without fear of reprisals from so-called musical experts.

1 Make friends with the pub dog, he'll introduce you to the best customers.
2 Don't pick fights with other dogs, it's easy to get banned from pubs.
3 Desist from bowel movements or 'territorial marking' in the pub garden.
4 Do not eat dog ends.
5 Try to get invited to the annual pub seaside outing – traditionally at Dognor Regis.

Sporting dogs should involve their masters in pub team games like cricket, bowls, Aunt Sally, skittles, darts, cribbage, cards, dominos etc. Teams tend to play away matches against other pubs. It'll get you out of the house and you'll meet other dogs in interesting new locations. If you are good at retrieving, your efforts will be richly rewarded at cricket match teas.

AT CLOSING TIME
(equivalent of going to your kennel).
1 Practice walking in a straight line.
2 Do not slur your bark, especially the *roa roa* sounds.
3 Do not get confused by your master's commands. This is merely altered speak, called 'drunkish'.
4 Allow plenty of time to get home.

You will need to stop at every other tree and lamppost.
5 When home, drink lots of water and go straight to bed. Get collar removed first.
6 Do not take sides during marital arguments.

NEXT DAY
If you feel ruff, take your master to the pub for a hair of the dog that bit you. You'll feel better. Check with the pub dog that you were discreet, i.e. did not try to mount, get into a dog fight, bite, snarl, urinate, or make a remark to the vicar about his collar.

♥♥♥♥♥♥♥♥♥♥♥♥♥♥♥♥♥♥♥
Editor
The 'Firkin' Brew Pubs have made us our own beer called Dogbolter which is very strong and suitable only for large dogs. Look out for 'Two Dogs' bottled drink, sweet but tasty.

♠♠♠♠♠♠♠♠♠♠♠♠♠♠♠♠♠♠♠

'Just you try bluffing with involuntary reflex actions like these.'

Biting Postmen

An unrepentant Mr Growler gets his teeth into the subject in depth

Why do we chase things? We don't know. We'll chase anything that moves – people, animals or vehicles. Most of us don't really mean any harm, it's all such great fun.

'Chase that car.'

For instance, we chase and corner a cat, then we let him go, it's the thrill of the chase, you see. However, there is something especially hackle-raising about Mr Mailman. Is it the dark blue uniform with that tantalising hint of red? Is it the parcels, mail sack, the string or rubber bands? Is it the Royal Warrant, the clang of the pillar-box door,

'Oh dear,' said the doctor, 'that ankle's going to need a stitch.'

the bicycle or van? Whatever, he's a human aniseed ball, a fang feast, a wicked tooth tormentor in blue serge. A letterbox luncheon.

MR GROWLER'S SELF-PRESERVATIONAL INSIDER TIPS

Being domesticated predatory pack animals, we jealously guard our territory which frankly is regularly invaded by delivery persons. OK, some of us do over-react. If you see a snarling, rigid growling stance, stand absolutely still, he thinks you're from an alien pack. Try puppyish whining to appeal to his mature instincts.

Now, body language, we dogs are heavily into it. This is the area where postmen go wrong (sorry, Mr Allen). These nervous tense, jerky types communicate the wrong profile (like showing us a raw steak). It's no good shouting 'Down boy' or 'Get down', then running. We *want* you to run, then we get you. And don't forget those giveaway pheromones, we can smell fear. You could get lucky.

Maybe an air balloon will fly over and you could slip away. No dog in the world can resist looking up at an air balloon and barking himself 'horse' as it were. Alternatively, always carry some aniseed balls (many of us are addicted to these, see page 96).

Here is a typical sequence of events:
1 Visitor approaches, wait for the soundbite.
2 We test reactions by barking and jumping up.
3 Wrong body language? We bite.
4 Friendly and confident?
   We reciprocate and lose interest.

5 Joggers, cyclists, animals, vehicles, stand no chance foolishly trying to outrun us.

The author is a Royal Mail specialist, racking up an impressive 572 bites, a UK record. He once concealed himself in a mailsack (which posties often leave lying around), was taken to the sorting depot and 'got' 33 postmen in one shift (and boy, did they shift). When bound over for psychiatric reports, the court heard that he suffers from red mists whenever he sees a postbox or Royal Mail van. *Mr Growler is a nom de chien.*

COMMUNICATION WORKERS UNION
ANNUAL CONFERENCE IN BOURNEMOUTH

DOG ATTACKS INCREASE AS UNION CALLS FOR NATIONAL REGISTRATION SCHEME

One in twenty delivery postal workers can expect to be attacked by a dog on their round this year and it is costing the Post Office millions in sick leave.

Figures released today show that reported dog attacks have increased to 5,975 this year - that is one attack every fifteeen working minutes - and that it resulted in 4,545 days sick taken by postal workers. The estimated cost to the Post Office of the sick days is two and a half million pounds and the cost to the Health service runs into tens of millions.

The Communication Workers Union is calling for a National Dog Registration Scheme along with the RSPCA so that owners can be made more responsible for the actions of their pets. Currently when attacks occur it is often impossible to identify the owner. If the attack occurs on private property, dogs do not have to be muzzled and most owners do not have their dogs insured.

Attacked more than 200 times in a 39 year career, George Allen, of Chagford, Devon, is Britain's most bitten postman.

"It is not the dogs I object to but the owners for not controlling them properly." says George. "Actually I am a dog lover and own one myself. My worst attack was from a Collie which tore all the muscles from my left arm. But I have had countless menaces."

ENDS

For more information contact:

Daniel Harris CWU Media/Campaigns
Tel: 0585 331 795
Tel: 01202 297 525 (conference press office.)

83

MR GROWLER'S CHASE 'N CATCH CHART

VICTIMS	EASY TO CATCH	LESS EASY	CHALLENGING	BITE
POSTMEN/MILKMEN	🐾			🐾 🐾 🐾 🐾
PAPERBOYS		🐾		🐾
CYCLISTS		🐾		🐾 🐾
JOGGERS	🐾			🐾 🐾
CARS/TRAINS			🐾	DON'T EVEN THINK OF IT
HARES/RABBITS			🐾	🐾 🐾
CATS		🐾	🐾	TOO DANGEROUS
SQUIRRELS			🐾	🐾 🐾

WE DETECT SPIRITS FROM THE SHADOWY WORLD OF THE SUPERNATURAL

HACKLES & TEMPERATURES RISE & FALL AS THE DOGBOLTERGEIST APPEARS

GHOSTLY FLICKERING IMAGES MATERIALISE IN THE ETHER

WE FORM A PICTURE OF THE APPARITION FROM THE 'OTHER SIDE'

HOW WE 'SEE' GHOSTS
ONLY MEDIUMS SHOULD TRY THIS AT HOME

To A Little Sick Boy!

Funny pictures
        on the wall,
Stories to be read
It really isnt
        bad at all
This being sick-abed!

Bone Burying Laid to Rest

From our industrial correspondent

ur primeval urges require us to bury food surpluses for later consumption. Mercifully few of us go hungry these days, thanks to our human pack friends. When given a bone which is difficult to break up and eat, our instincts tell us to bury it for later. Many flat-dwelling dogs fed on canned food never have the chance to bury leftovers and can be seen trying to phantom-bury their dish in a corner. But give that same dog a bone in a garden and he'll dig a hole with his front paws, drop the bone in from his jaw, push the soil back and flatten it with his snout, just as dogs have done since time immemorial. This will fool scavengers and be delicious to eat later. That's the way we figure it anyway.

TOP TEN DOG JOBS

(source PAWSIE Job Index).
Bones are highly sought-after commodities. As such the best jobs revolve around ossiferous occupations which are self-explanatory and carry their own rewards.

1   Cemetery/Undertaker
2   * Butcher
3   * Restaurant
4   * Glue Factory
5   * Bonemeal Processor
6   * Abbatoir
7   Archaeology/Palaeontology
8   Catacomb operative
9   Satanist
10 Bone Commodity Broker
    (in common parlance, a rag and bone person)
    * =FTSE 100 Index Industries

Editor

The bare bones of it is that we carry out these jobs without the help of tools. Another reason why dogs are superior to humans.

HEY... HOW ABOUT THAT BONE?

TOP DOG JOB SPOT

News just came in concerning an archaeological expedition in search of an elephants' graveyard. They are looking for diggers. *And they ban us from The Natural History Museum!*

86

The Editor
The Happy Dog Book
Berkshire

**If you've
a bone to pick,
scratch us a line.**

**Aggrieved of The Gravediggers Arms,
Rectory Lane, Rottingdean**
We've had heavy rain lately and bones often come to the surface in our village graveyard. I was gnawing an old arm bone behind the flying buttresses when a widow visited her recently deceased husband's grave. The crunching noises must have upset her because she entirely misconstrued the situation and reported me to the sexton. But surely they know that it couldn't have been his bones. We dogs always wait a decent amount of time, until the coffin has rotted that is.

Editor
A case of sense of humerus failure!

Digger from Bury St Edmonds writes
Being a rectory dog, I see a lot of burials in our churchyard. I admit, I do unearth a lot of bones in God's acre and of course bury them again for later, as you do. I know it's wrong because when caught there is always a dreadful fuss. I'm thrashed and locked in the crypt. But answer me this. Why is it that the vicar, the curate and the gravediggers spend all that time, effort and money re-consecrating the bones when they must know that I would bury them again anyway for nothing?

Editor
We get a lot of letters from hounds in your position. Vicars and the like are of course in the business of denying temptation, but modern life should be about recycling. After all, bones deep beneath the ground are no good to man nor...one would have thought the ecclesiastical outlook to be less severe, especially from dog-collar wearing clergy.

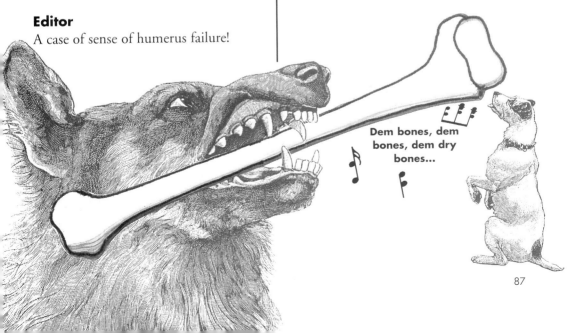

Dem bones, dem bones, dem dry bones...

**From T. Bonesteak,
Boneshaker Lane, Bucks.**

I'm a dog in a bonemeal factory. Canine heaven you may think. Yes, but it's also heartbreaking. The other day I found out what happens to the mountains of bones that are delivered here. They are crushed and wait for it, spread on fields in the countryside! So many hungry and deserving dogs in the world, and all they do is give foxes something to sniff.

Editor

This issue is a real bone of contention in the canine world.

**From Fossil,
Pleistocine Way, Plymouth**

I've spent days digging in the graveyard next to our garden but all I ever find are small urns. These crematoria shouldn't be allowed. I feel sorry for the foxes, maggots and worms, let alone us dogs.

Editor

Too bone idle to bury corpses, they burn them instead. But they are operating with a skeleton staff due to cut-backs.

Belgrave, writes from The Gatekeeper's House, Civic Cemetery, Gravesend

My master gave me a good strapping the other day when he found some bones that I'd buried. He says it's unethical, but I saw him put some bones in the dustbin after last Sunday's lunch. Where did he get those from, eh?

Editor

A clear case of blatant hypocrisy, no bones about it.

● ● ● ● ● ● ● ● ● ● ● ● ● ● ● ● ● ●

From Admiral, The Jolly Roger, Cornwall (retired sea dog)

We seem to be fresh out of pirates down here – something to do with the exercise men hounding them out or something like that, so they say. It's all wrong. The only way to get to the beach was down their secret tunnels and in my day it gladdened the heart to see the Skull & Crossbones flying in the breeze, as we embarked for the Skeleton Coast with me on dog watch.

Editor

You'd be a dead dog if Blind Pew gave you the...you don't have black spots on your coat, do you?

● ● ● ● ● ● ● ● ● ● ● ● ● ● ● ● ● ●

From Meddler, a Protestant Dog, name and address withheld

Our new lady vicar is a vegetarian. It can't be right that she's allowed to bury people can it?

Editor

Rightly, you've a bone to pick with her reverence. She should turn over a new leaf.

43

The Hound of the Baskervilles

From Sherlock, The Holmes, Baskerville Moor, Devonshire

I thought I'd go in for a spot of ghost hunting in our local haunted garden of remembrance. My feet turned to marrow-bone jelly when a ghostly slavering giant hell-hound appeared and tried to lick me.

Editor

We all go through this inquisitive stage, but best to avoid burial places at night. Our supernatural, paranormal, psychic powers are well known, but lick you, I'm surprised he had the ghoul!

Watchdog Bono Fido Case History
Held at the Supreme Court of Justice

DEFENDANT
Cuddly Soft Toys Inc.,
Dogsville, Delaware

DEFENCE
Conducted by Attorney Virginia
Foxhound

PROSECUTION
District Dog Attorney

PLAINTIFF
Campaign For Real Dogs

WITNESS
Deputy Dawg

HEARD BEFORE
Judge Mental Aberration, motto
'Injustice shall be done'

**'Another fine dog mess you got me into,
Stanley.'**

CHARGE
That the use of inanimate fluffy toys in
publicity material constitutes: unfair
substitution; unfair dismissal; loss of
employment, hearth, home and
affection; denial of our uncivil
liberties and animal rights.

VERDICT
Victory for CFRD

JUDGEMENT
That Exhibit A be replaced with Exhibit B

PRESS REPORTS
*'The collective bite of CFRD triumphed
over polyester, rayon and ribbons.
Animal wrongs righted.'*

'Who says our legislation lacks teeth.'

'CFRD wins the legal scrap.'

Favourite TV Programmes

A dog's life can be enriched by watching the transmission of visible moving images by electromagnetic wireless waves with synchronised sound signals, suggests our scientific expert Logie, a Bairded Collie, who writes in language even a puppy can understand.

There are 400 million dogs worldwide: 53 million in the USA, 6.55 million in the UK, 3.8 million in Australia.

UK viewing figures:
54% watch television.
36% don't watch TV.
Ratings: Could be 36% better.

Editor
Oh for Dog's sake get on with it.

Logie speaks.
It is to the 36% that I address this article and say to you, you don't know what you're missing. I urge you (yes, I know you have your own) to take an afternoon off by yourself and switch on the television. Accomplish this by pressing your paw against the button usually located top right. If you cannot reach, jump up and head-butt the switch. There is a black plastic thing with which to change channels (it has no name) but it's too complicated to use. Don't bite it,

'Me? I've had lots of rolls.'

the screen goes fuzzy. Draw the curtains with your teeth. Now you can settle down in the best sofa and enjoy.

The image should be in colour (a waste on humans) although there will be black and white films too. (They can see these better.)

Resist looking behind the set to see what's happened. You have to understand that everything happens at the front. Don't lick the screen, even if Lassie comes on, or fog it with your breath.

'Rolf! Rolf! Rolf!'

Puppies, do not have 'accidents' on the live wires. Don't go for a drink during the breaks, you might miss a dog-food commercial. You can sing along to the music without fear of reprisal. Cover your eyes with your paws should violent or noisy material be transmitted.

Surveys show the following to be the most popular viewing.

DOGUMENTARIES

Healing, psychic, care, sporting, working dogs etc.

TV COMMERCIALS

Andrex Toilet Tissue, Dulux Dog, HMV Dog.

GENERALLY

Cookery programmes, wildlife dogumentaries, anything with animals, choral or church choir programmes.

Sparky MacNab, a West Highland Terrier rescue dog, is a TV addict. He sits for long periods with his nose inches from the screen waiting for interesting material to... well, materialise. He relishes the sight of most of God's creatures – birds and animals, but is a bit snooty about amphibians, like tortoises and the ilk. Sparky would make a great TV researcher or censor, but is probably too emotional to become a serious critic because when the Andrex puppy appears, he licks the screen and tries to climb inside the set, crying with frustration at the same time. He loves any animated film including, curiously, The Muppets. Other favourites are One Man and His Dog, about sheep dog trials, which gets him very worked up. Others in the top three are Come Outside (he's in love with Pippin), and Animal Hospital. When Sparky watched a video of The Brinkstone Fox (about a fox cub brought up by a pack of foxhounds), he was jumping about the room from chair to chair in a high state of excitement. Lucky it wasn't the local cinema.

'Look, Sparkie, the
TV transmitter's up there'.

SPECIFICALLY

Animal Hospital

Animal Magic

Casualty Dogs

Emmerdale Farm

Hollywood Pets

It's a Vet's Life

Pet Power

Songs of Praise

Zoo Quest

FAVOURITE FILMS

The Incredible Journey

Lady and the Tramp

Old Yeller

101 Dalmations

The Shaggy Dog

The Fox and the Hound

Hercule & Sherlock

Any animated cartoon film with Goofy

Pluto or Gromit

Any Lassie or Rin Tin Tin film

Confessions of the Aniseed Bitch of Hollywood

The CHESTER CHESAPEAKE celebrity interview with SOPHIA, the aniseed queen – the all-American Cocker Spaniel

WHAT THE AMERICAN PRESS SAY ABOUT CHESTER

'No-one muzzles or mauls Chester.'
Hoboken Mail

'Chester Chesapeake is a fearless newshound, never out of his depth even in deep and sometimes ruff water.'
The Hollywood Reporter

'If there are facts to be found or stories to be sniffed, Chester the Chesapeake Bay Retriever will find them.'
Maryland Monitor

'He's one hell of a son of a gun.'
Variety

'To him, interviewing is like hunting duck – you're a sitting one and he is pointing at you.'
The Swampmarsh Times

'Don't even think about putting him off the scent, he never gives up.'
Cesspit Quarterly

C Chester **S** Sophia

C You're a gun dog like me, doggone it, we speak the same language.

S *Not quite, Chester, you're descended from a Newfie after all.*

C They call you SOPHIA SO GOOD, the good-time girl.

S *Sure, they call me Queen too. I'm from a very old Boston family. My ancestral grandmother Obo Obo came over from England in 1880.*

C You're hounded by the packarazzi, you run with the rat pack, there was the affair with the Boston Terrier...and now the aniseed addiction rap, the 3 dollar a day habit.

S *I see why they call you fearless Chester. Listen, there are two things that make a Hollywood bitch's life worth living.*
1 A stud dog.
2 Pimpenella anisum or aniseed to you, and all my habits are expensive.

C You don't deny it then?

S *Put it this way, I'm not a jealous Jezebel but I'd swap places with any hound out there from the Middle East or Mediterranean areas where they grow rolling acres of the stuff. Thanks to the Romans (great dog lovers), it grows in Northern Europe from where early settlers*

brought it here to North America, Dog bless them.

C What is aniseed?

S *It's a popular spice plant, about dog height – 2 feet or 60 cms. Creamy flowers appear in summer and later those divine seeds are formed – seeds of content, I call them, and boy do I sow them.*

C What's it used for?

S *For flavouring cakes and candies and liqueurs like Pastis, Pernod, Ricard, Ouzo, Raki and Arrak.*

C If I may interrupt, it sounds like a class A drug.

S *Chester, it's also used in medicine for gastric and respiratory disorders, tension, overactivity and flatulence – I think you should take some.*

C How do you know all this?

S *By sniffing, we tell everything by sniffing, you should know that.*

C What does it taste like, what is the effect?

S *In the form of aniseed balls it's lickerish heaven – the planet Pluto. To paraphrase Tom Wolfe, it's your Kandy-Koloured Tangerine Aniseed-Flake Streamline Baby. See, I was educated.*

C Do the Enforcement Agencies know about this stuff?

S *Yearhh, and they ensure the stuff gets grown, them and the Department of Agriculture, it's not illegal, you know.*

C Any mob connections?

S *Not mob, more pack – the candy stores get packed.*

C Who are these shadowy dealers?

S *There's CANDID KANDIES on the sunny side of Sunset. Then, MADAME JAR JARS on Wilshire, SWEET DREAMS on Beverly Boulevard and SUGAR-COATED ALLSORTS on Malibu Drive.*

C How is it sold?

S *Balls are weighed carefully on scales and sold by the ounce.*

C How long does a hit last?

S *About 3 minutes, but they are highly addictive.*

C Do you snort it or what?

S *No, it's not to be sniffed at, you suck the balls very slowly. Here try one, Chester.*

C Thanks...um, that's very good...very, very good...wonderful...marvellous... wow...give me another...quick...

● ● ● ● ● ● ● ● ● ● ● ● ● ● ● ● ● ● ●   The interview tails off.

99

Howling along Down Under

From our musical correspondent, Maestro 'Moggy Munsterlander'

1. Sit comfortably
2. Throw head well back
3. Ululate – howl and wail
4. Give it all you've got – cry wolf
5. Try to bark in tune
6. To perfect your timing, wag your tail four times before starting
7. Aspire to the melodic talents of the New Guinea Singing Dog*
8. Locate other howlers, form a pack, look for a recording contract

Once, musical evenings and family sing-songs were the primary form of entertainment, especially for outback communities. That was before television. Many pets reasoned that this was a 'right-on' situation. A 'let's-get-on-down, song of the tribe, join me to bring the pack together', type anthem.

This is what happens in our minds.
'Great, a sing-song, they do understand about reinforcing pack cohesion after all.'

The human mind.
'Shut that awful row up, or I'll feed you to the goannas, you flea-ridden cur.'

We dogs are very musical and love nothing better than to join in. Bearing in mind that our musical ear is far better than theirs, it is baffling to be compared to Tasmanian Devils undergoing torture. We scholars of Offenbark know all about tone deafness! My advice is to ignore the heathen, cultureless so-and-so's and follow this posture and vocalisation sequence.

Take the lead from an American group called The Canine Chorus who will sing-bark *Happy Birthday to You* in a variety of styles, like blues, pop and country and western, etc. I wonder if they've recorded the romantic C&W ballad by a man to his wife, entitled 'I'd take you to the dog show, but I'm afraid you might win.' The Canine Chorus have unfortunately started to record with cats. Gut instinct tells me that this is a mistake.

MRS. DALMATIAN

MRS. DALMATIAN

*Editor *This is a dog from...er... New Guinea...who sings...er...melodically although I haven't actually heard one myself.*

'On lead...'

Look out for these sure-fire, larynx-loosening trigger sounds and images.

- Anyone practising the violin, zither, bagpipes or trumpet
- Opera singers
- Choirs, rare out here, but try the Church
- Christmas carols, especially '*A Dog in a Manger*'
- The moon. Good for canine choral baying.

MASTER SEALYHAM

MASTER SEALYHAM

MRS MONGREL

MRS. MONGREL

TOP TEN SINGALONG TUNES

Neighbours theme

Home and Away theme

Coronation Street theme

Eastenders theme

Old Macdonald Had a Farm

Lazy Bones

No Bananas

How Much is that Doggy in the Window

You Ain't Nothing but a Hound Dog

Dem bones, dem bones, dem dry bones

Plus anything by Rolf Harris.

Unholy Matrimony

'*Dearly beloved, we are gathered here today in the eyes of Dog, to join this bitch to this old dog.*' (But only in France or Japan.) Humans have a romantic notion of tying the knot (and we know all about ties, knots and being hitched). But we're not like them. Swans and elephants mate for life but for us a marriage of convenience lasting an hour is about right. Those incurable romantics, the French, have a marriage bureau in Toulouse charging £60 for four introductions using a computerised system detailing temperament and breed details. It is a 'civil ceremony', performed by the vet.

The Japanese go further offering a wedding/honeymoon/reception. Wedded bliss continues after the nuptials in a $9,000 doghouse, kitted out with non-stop videos, Four Paws cologne and bubble bath. Cordon bleu food is served (well, Poodles like it) or American-style barbecue food. Not off the leash yet, the happy couple can celebrate anniversaries in a dog hotel at a mere $165 a day!

Japanese dogs love travel (it gets them out of those tiny apartments), and cameras. Now they can jet'n snap away (those fighting dogs are a menace), at Jackson's Dog Spa, Orlando, Florida. Luxurious treatments are offered to make them feel like emperors – soothing music by Bark, whirlpool baths, massage with aromatherapy oils and sunlamps if the sun doesn't shine. Part of the attraction for these working breeds are the juicy bones which make such a change from raw fish and rice.

'I'LL TELL HIM I'VE GOT A HEADACHE.'

'PERHAPS SHE'S NOT ON HEAT.'

'NO, THAT TV DINNER GAVE ME TERRIBLE WIND.'

'HAPPY, DARLING?'

Mating attempts with Humans

By our breeding correspondent, freelance newshound, Randy Dandy Dinmont

It beats me why humans react so violently when we male dogs try to mate with their legs, or to be honest, their arms, elbows or knees. But why are they so surprised? It's as rare as a sirloin steak to meet a bitch on heat, so what is a poor dog to do?

I know we're on a good hiding to nothing, but as a substitute activity it takes a lot of beating, if you'll pardon the expression. As an attention-seeking device it works beautifully. We get the attention of RUNS and BCWS*, with kicks and verbal abuse thrown in. Look, I know we're not fussy but when that which cannot be denied, is denied, watch out. Humans must understand our frustrations. Powerful urges are at work here, whole hosts of hormones climactically surging and thrusting. If they appreciated this and let us among our own kind, then all would be well. Until then, no-one is safe, not the family cat or any other dog, not your favourite fluffy toy, cushion or anything that stays still long enough.

In a way, humans are our own kind, our adopted pack. We share food, dens, grooming, play, rituals and territorial patrols. But to be honest, humans don't smell right for us – sexually, if you know what I mean – no disrespect. Now, a bitch in season...but you wouldn't know about that. Admittedly it could be a different story if homo sapiens was still on four legs, like us (and stories have reached me from night-clubbing dogs in Damascus), but frankly it wouldn't be satisfactory. It's all in the nose with us dogs, that and the ano-genital licking of course.

We do appreciate that our surrogate activities cause embarrassment, especially to women, and yes, we often get carried away, but please, no hard feelings.

*Rolled-up Newspaper Syndrome and Bucket of Cold Water Syndrome

Why Legs?

Un-dog-like and awkward they may be, but they are:

1 Accessible.

2 Easy to grasp.

3 Sensuous if unclad, especially hairy legs.

4 In plentiful supply, supplemented by house visitors.

5 Firm and rigid, like a dachshund on tip toe.

6 Because they are there.

Reproduced by kind permission of Private Eye.

Going for the Crotch

(embracing bottom licking)

A celebration of ano-genital sniffing

'Not much of a party, only two men and a dog.'

'Hm, nice houndstooth check...'

When we meet other dogs, we don't say, 'Hi, my name is Rusty from 27 Fazakerley Way, belonging to Mrs Sulaman the Magnificent. I'm an eight year-old pariah dog who's just been de-wormed and castrated but still suffering from rectal boils for which I'm taking suppositories, and by the way, I've just had a dead stoat for dinner,' (or whatever they say in polite society). No, no need. We can tell all that from ano-genital sniffing. You may have noticed that when two dogs meet, they stand head-to-tail and sniff each others' rears. The upright tails quiver slightly. This squeezes the anal glands and releases strong-smelling odours acting as chemical information laboratories, telling us all we need to know.

PHEROMONES SUBLIME

When we meet humans, we use the same techniques, heh, we're dogs! Women are easiest. Most muzzles can slip up a skirt. Dobermans are best at it, being crotch height and not easy to push away. Because Golden Retrievers are lovable dogs, there is a reluctance to deter them.

'You promised not to go for Father's crutch.'

Mind you, women do struggle. If only they'd let us carry out our analysis in peace before shouting about gender discrimination. Men are just as bad, but the signals are less clear through their trousers. They are basically frightened that we will bite their testicles off (fair enough, I suppose, and justified, especially if they try RUNS* on us). We do need time for a good sniff though, and here's what we can learn:

1 She's on heat/not on heat
2 She's pregnant/not pregnant
3 She's recently mated/not mated
4 She's looking for a mate or not (pheromones you see, like a slosh of French perfume to us).
5 Her age
6 What she had for breakfast
7 She's apprehensive (or not)
8 Any physical infirmities

Believe you me, if a tracker dog can detect two ounces of explosive in a sealed jar, dipped in paraffin, encased in a cubic foot of concrete, this is absolutely no problem for us. It's all in the nose, you see.

I know what you are thinking, that we're just a pack of randy mongrels. But you mustn't give a dog a bad name and hang him. Listen, we're only trying to get to know you. That, and looking for your anal glands just inside your rectum, as us dogs do (they are pea sized, one each side and delicious to lick). And, OK, it's true, we are banned from nudist camps!

* Rolled-Up Newspaper Syndrome

'Well, I don't call it heaven when we're not allowed to sniff each others' bottoms.'

Why dogs are superior to humans

But please don't think that we're rubbing your noses in it

A Saint Bernard can tell if a buried avalanche victim is alive just by sniffing the snow. How? He has a nasal heat detector, an infra-red device called the Jacobsens Organ. This was discovered by a Dr Zotterman of Sweden (he sounds like one of us).

'Boy, you're ugly.'

'Ssssh, those dogs will hear us.'

'It's for off-peak calls.'

We can orienteer home from hundreds of miles away, or find our owners who, say, have travelled to a destination unknown to us by bus, train, and boat. How? We don't know, but we can.

We routinely predict thunderstorms and earthquakes by changes in barometric pressure, air flow and currents with our special touch-sensitive hairs.

We know when our owner is coming home long before he arrives. Psychic?

Nawww, we can hear his footfalls or car engine. It's nothing really, after all a wolf can hear another wolf howling from four miles away.

Our owners believe we can detect ghosts and the subsequent temperature changes. Maybe we can, why give all your secrets away?

'Can you hear that, dear?'

We can hear rats, mice and bats (we used to eat them in the wild), with our ultrasonic hearing abilities. Ask any sheepdog.

Whippet Racing

The Shepherd's Dog

'I've got this whistling in my ear.'

Wolves can detect deer scent from one and a half miles away. (Well, it keeps the wolf from the door.)

Greyhounds are the fastest dogs on earth, the record speed being 41.83 mph followed closely by whippets who can average 37 mph over 150 yards.

Our eyes shine in the dark because we have an image intensifying layer at the back of our eyes and can see in the dark.

We have a range and field of vision of 250 degrees (better than yours at 180 degrees), and are sensitive to movement up to a mile away, although your binocular vision is better.

Impressed? Let me tell you, that's nothing. It's our sense of smell which is truly amazing. Without wishing to make you feel inadequate (no, I'm not a Saluki), our olfactory organs are 250,000 times more sensitive than yours. Why? Because you have 5 million smell sensitive cells as opposed to our 220 million. Lots of people try to outsmart us, including drug traffickers, escaped terrorists and canine researchers.

'I should win by a hare, but I wouldn't bet on it.'

For instance, the latter have tried on us:

THE GLASS SLIDE TEST

One of a set of slides is touched by a human fingertip. The slides are then put away for six weeks and then taken out again. The test dog can tell which slide was touched.

Editor

And they bar us from The Magic Circle!

THE PEBBLE TEST

Six men pick up and throw a pebble as far as possible. The test dog sniffs the hand of one man then finds and retrieves his pebble!

Marijuana, cocaine and heroin have characteristic odours which smugglers go to enormous lengths to disguise, using encapsulation, tanks of gasoline, mothballs, onions, perfume, pepper, garlic and chocolate even. All to no avail, pathetic really.

Bloodhounds can follow a trail 100 miles long and four days old, in the right cool moist conditions. The butyric acid found in sweat from feet is so strong that sleuthing is easy. He can tell an individual amongst many, where all wore shoes. An

THE ACME " SILENT " WHISTLE.

escaped prisoner can put on rubber boots or a lost child can ride a bicycle, but a hound will still find that person, using crushed vegetation as an additional clue. Our discerning nose is a million times more sweat responsive than yours. This is a blessing, I assure you, although we gather that humans are not as keen on feet smells as we.

Any dog can detect one drop of blood in 5 quarts of water or a bone buried 2 feet underground.

We can sense or smell the odour of illness long before it happens to our masters-impending heart attacks, seizure, epilepsy or depressive sickness.

Bomb squad dogs can detect Semtex, sulphur in gunpowder, acid in nitro-glycerine or oil on concealed weapons.

An American Army tracker dog once found an ounce of explosive sealed in a jar dipped in liquid paraffin, buried in a square metre of concrete.

Windsor Castle used dogs to find wet and dry rot lurking behind panelling and plaster and under floors. The workdogs were a Collie, a Labrador and a Springer Spaniel Cross.

Editor

Surely they should have been Rottweilers. The sort of place where your regal bow comes in handy.

In Ontario, Canada, German Shepherds working in sub-zero temperatures found 150 leaks in a 100-mile long natural gas pipeline 18 feet underground.

Human personal odour is genetically inherited. We can identify individual family members but we can't tell identical twins apart, because they have the same body scent. We'll strut our stuff when cloning comes along.

So you see, we can be trained to find or detect any substance or smell, and I mean any. It doesn't even matter if we are blind and deaf, the world is still a wonderful, though smelly, place for us. Dry rot and truffles (both fungi), insect infestation behind walls (we can smell the methane gas – yes really), it's all the same to us and more or less any dog can do it.

Editor

And they sometimes try to put us down!

Dumbfounded? Well, listen to this. William H. Montgomery was preparing his boat for a fishing trip in New England on September 10, 1938. He whistled for his Red Setter, Redsey, but the dog refused to jump aboard. The weather was perfect, but Redsey stood firmly on the dock, barking. Mr Montgomery was suspicious and postponed his departure. One hour later, a violent gale blew up, smashing boats and coastal buildings. The great hurricane of 1938 lasted 12 days, killed 600 people, and caused 250 million dollars worth of damage. It was the first hurricane in the area for 70 years. Redsey - what a hero!

Paddy, a Golden Retriever, was swept off a boat in the Straits of Florida. It took him 5 days to swim 15 miles to a beach in Key West, losing 15 lb in the process.

Floyd is a National Dog Support Group dog who works in Maidstone prison. He is trained to sniff out drugs, explosives, arms and ammunition. The Black Labrador watches visitors file past him. If he detects drugs on someone, he stands in front of them. So far he has searched 11,000 visitors and indicated 47 of them. His biggest haul was £75,000 worth of heroin which the prisoner would have sold for £500,000. Various breeds are used for this work, among them Labradors, Collies, Spaniels and German Shepherds.

Ronnie Fraser, the recently deceased British character actor, apparently turned up at his local Belsize Park police station one night after a few drinks, and asked to see the sergeant. 'Ah, Mr Fraser, what can I do for you?' 'Well,' says Ronnie, 'do you have one of those sniffer dogs here? You see, I've lost my stash!'

111

Keeping humans as pets

By our Lifestyle editor

'We take it in turns until we get another dog.'

It's hard work owning a member of homo sapiens, but mutually rewarding in terms of enjoying companionship, protection and security. Your surrogate partnership offers something on which to lavish love. He'll make an excellent pet for your puppies. Try to spend as much quality time as possible with him, he'll get lonely if left alone at home. Remember, he is a creature in his own right, don't anthropomorphise.

Follow these tips to ensure strong teeth, glossy shiny hair and a wet nose.

• Make sure he realises that you are the pack leader. Be cruel to be kind. Aspire to winning a Kennel Club Good Citizen award. • Encourage good behaviour through obedience and socialisation training. • Try motivation training. Reward with praise and chocolate biscuits. • Watch for signs of unsociable behaviour – mounting, urinating, fighting,

BOB'S KENNELS

'I know it saves on day care, but I still don't feel entirely comfortable...'

'Don't worry dear, it's probably just puppy fat.'

RGJ

chewing slippers, shredding bedding material, biting the hand that feeds him or the furniture. • Break up fights by inserting a claw/paw into the rectum – then he can be safely led away. • Take out a pet insurance policy that additionally covers boarding kennel fees should you be indisposed. • Make sure he doesn't stray. All pets should have an ID tattoo on the ear or a microchip implant, plus identity tag and collar (with the exception of gentlemen of the cloth, they are generally lax in this area). • Watch for signs of obesity like wolfing down food. Give him plenty of daily exercise – running, jogging, walking, swimming. Keep him amused with retrieving games and tough bouncy toys. Whilst alone at home, stimulate him with cardboard boxes, ramps, tunnels and jumps. • When free running in the countryside, prevent him from worrying farm animals or he may be legally shot. If unsure, keep him on a lead. • Ensure regular general

'The Clergyman' Dog Collar

health checks for common ailments like fleas, incontinence, mange or worms. Watch, or smell, for excessive wind, loose stools or dull skin. • A balanced diet is essential for anal control. He or she needs vitamins, protein, mineral supplements and fresh grass or vegetables. • Digestive system OK? Try to avoid vegetarian food, this will cause flatulence. Do not let him foul footpaths or parks. • Groom him daily and brush his teeth, if he'll let you. The gums should be a healthy pink colour. Check for bad breath and plaque. • Homeopathic remedies relieve scratching and itching. Try inserting a suppository of Viper's-bugloss when he gets listless and Belladonna tablets if he becomes aggressive. • Discourage him from sleeping on your bed. • Clip his nails regularly. • It's always distressing to have to put a pet down, but the vet will take care of this painlessly should injury, illness or old age demand.

'What if he was only playing dead?'

-PILBROW-

Coming out of the closet

Dotty, a canine connosewer, lifts the lid on drinking lavatory bowl water.

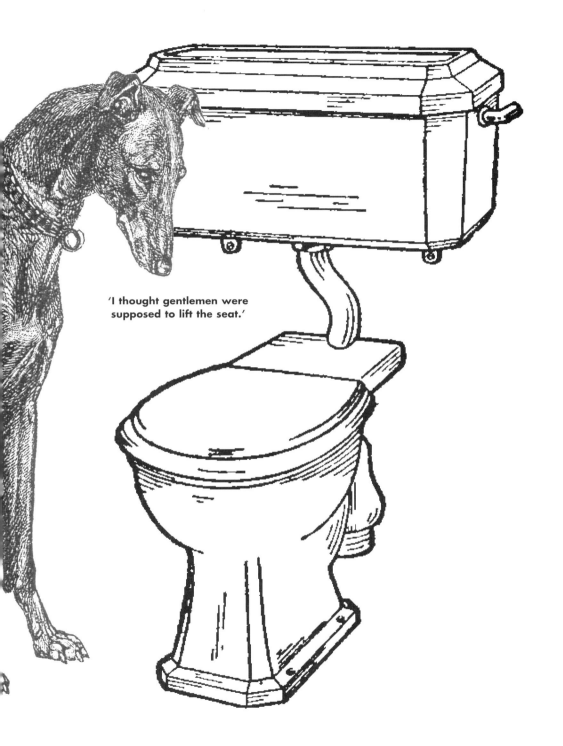

'I thought gentlemen were supposed to lift the seat.'

W e're opportunists, right. When we're thirsty, we don't think, 'It's a lovely day, why don't I trot down to the municipal fountain and get a cool refreshing draught of clean, sparkling H_2O.' No, we must have it now. There's always a lavatory bowl somewhere in a house, so bingo. (My first male friend was called Bingo.)

The small Water Spaniel, perfect for the job.

And another thing. We like water. We like to splash and roll in it. You can't do that in a dog bowl, so what's a dog to do indoors? It's obvious, the toilet bowl. You can really sink a muzzle into that cool porcelain on a hot day, then have a thoroughly good shake after slaking one's thirst. We're not fussy, you see. A flushed 'can', as the Americans say (I like that, it reminds me of dog food), is just as legitimate as the village pond.

Good to see these young pups getting into bad habits so early in life.

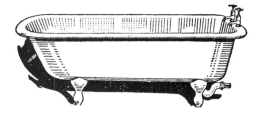

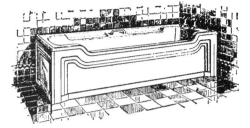

'We French know how to live.'

You know about our amazing sense of smell and you know we like strong tastes. Is it all beginning to make sense to you now? Well, it's the same with water, here are our favourite slurps: **1** Brackish pond water complete with, eh hum, lowly pond life. **2** Muddy puddles. **3** Beer. **4** Sewage farm water. **5** Cattle trough water. Believe you me, if, day after day, you're given tap water in your bowl – that tasteless, bland, re-cycled, sanitised, filtered rubbish – then lavatory water is like a breath of foul air. We lap it up. It's strong, tasty, colourful with a good after-taste. Sometimes malty, mellow, distinctive, often slightly tawny or straw coloured with discernible aromas of caramel and hints of sulphur. How's that for an educated nose?

Editor

What erudition, and they call us ignorant hounds!

The tastes vary enormously. Never the same twice, sometimes acidic, sometimes a palette dominated by rankness. Whatever did dogs do before Mr Thomas Crapper came on the scene? He certainly improved the quality of our lives, but you never see humans celebrating him with a lap of honour, as it were.

There are disadvantages when we come out of the closet. Humans dislike: 1 Pawmarks on the porcelain. 2 Sharing facilities with us. 3 Getting the toilet paper wet. 4 Scratch marks on the seat. Watch out for potential dangers: 1 Falling in if you are small 2 Don't drink blue water. This is disinfectant. 3 Flick the ENGAGED sign in public toilets. You will then not be disturbed. 4 Whilst pushing the seat up with your nose, watch out for the backward pivot.

Dotty, a freelance mongrel, is presently being counselled at the world-famous Dundrinkin Detention Centre, Lapland.

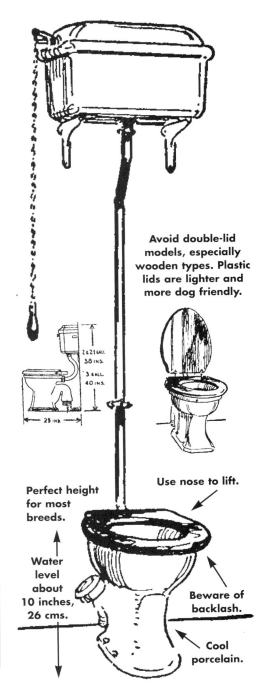

Avoid double-lid models, especially wooden types. Plastic lids are lighter and more dog friendly.

Use nose to lift.

Perfect height for most breeds.

Water level about 10 inches, 26 cms.

Beware of backlash.

Cool porcelain.

Working like a dog

A serious-ish article

Many of us have a very strong work ethic and inbred traits that are useful for work. We are happiest when our talents are used fully, be it guarding, racing, rescue, sled or draught work. In the dim (don't talk to me about Afghans) and distant past, most breeds performed some task but in the main they are now just companions to their owners. True sporting and working breeds are as follows:

GUNDOGS Pointer, Retriever, Spaniel.
HERDING German Shepherd, Corgi, Lancashire Heeler, Maremma, Collie. (We often need to herd human families – they stray, you know.)
HOUNDS Scent: Bloodhound, Basset, Beagle. Eyesight: Greyhound, Saluki, Mastiff. All talented at running down large and small prey.

TERRIERS Skilled at going to ground to hunt and flush out vermin like the fox from his lair or drive game. Noisy, energetic, sporty and nippy.
TOY BREEDS Make splendid guard dogs, showing great courage. Chihuahuas can overcome and kill cockroaches, I think ...(stupid boys, says it all), whilst Toy Yorkshire Terriers, the smallest dogs of all, were once fearless rodent killers.

Our undisputed talents have been, eh humm, exploited, but we don't really mind. To tell the truth, there's a lot more we can do, given that the world to us is a primordial soup of smells, a visual feast, and a whispering gallery of sounds (most of which are inaudible to you lot). We do appreciate that some of us are work shy (heh, what's wrong with sleeping). However, as things are, we publish here

'Who says you can't teach an old dog new tricks?'

INTRODUCING 'SPOT' THE AMAZING CANINE CANNONBALL

for the first time, a list of jobs which young pups might like to consult.

COMMUNITY CARE

Guide Dogs for the Blind; Dogs for the Disabled; Hearing Dogs for the Deaf; Children in Hospital and Animal Therapy (stroking for stress reduction); Pro-active Therapy Dogs and Care Dogs

And on your left is St Paul's Cathedral designed by Sir Christopher Wren in 1675 and built over a period of 35 years.

'Wow, that's some guide dog!'

(e.g. aids to psychotherapy, detection of onset of epileptic fits, diabetes, heart attack, seizures, depressive illness); Project Safe Run hires out trained dogs to run alongside female joggers in Paris, so far with a 100% success rate.

COUNTRY PURSUITS

Sheep herding, farm and stable, truffle hunting, rabbiting, hunting, fishing and retrieving.

MOUNTAIN RESCUE INSURANCE POLICY

SUB-ZERO/MOUNTAIN RESCUE

Saint Bernard. (In the 17th century an English artist depicted a Saint Bernard with a cask around its neck after rescuing a traveller on the Italian-Swiss border. In reality they never carry one.)

Estrela, Pyrenean, Bernese Mountain Dogs.

Collies, Alsatians and Labradors are used in the Scottish Highlands by the Search and Rescue Dog Association. They have

XXX SERVE YOURSELF

'The St Bernard has lost the franchise.'
Reproduced by permission of Punch Ltd. Cartoon by Ken Allen

to be winched down during emergency helicopter missions in severe weather conditions. Dogs can cover the ground that otherwise 40 people would, with the additional dimension of smell to aid them.

Editor

*By rights, Basenji and Telomian should be on this list. You can't accuse them of barking because they can't. Instead, they **yodel** – yes truly! Only drawback is that the former comes from the African Congo and the Telomian from Malaysia where they live in houses on stilts – just a thought though.*

'It's true, dogs *do* make the best burglar alarms.'

SLEDGING AND HARNESS

Greenlands, Eskimo Dogs, Samoyeds, Malamutes, Huskies, Akitas.

ARMED SERVICES/EMERGENCY SERVICES

HM Customs & Excise (drug sniffers)
Rescue Services (confined spaces work)
Detection of arson accelerants (Fire Brigade)

Army attack dogs, parachuting and behind enemy lines, penetration
Regimental mascots
Police work generally, including finding bodies under water ('Reservoir Dogs')
Security work (guarding)
Prison Service (tracking, drug and firearms detection)

'You can't beat a Doberman for sussing out intruders.'

OFFICE

This task probably suits smaller breeds but nevertheless is the cushiest around. We are allowed to sleep on the job. All we have to do is sort out the bulldog clips and soothe the executive brow by relieving stress. Not bad eh? Remember Laika the mongrel bitch in Sputnik 2? Now that's really hard work operating all those computers up amongst Sirius and Procyon, the dog-stars. I'd swop her Order of Lenin any day for a pastrami on rye at lunchtime.

SPORTING

Racing, Hunting.

SHOW BUSINESS

Circus (performing)
Acting, talking, singing (voice-over work etc.)
Hypnotism *

*Oscar, the black Labrador, works the university entertainment circuit with his human assistant. Volunteers come on stage and stare into his unusually big, dark, bulgy eyes. Soon they are in a deep hypnotic trance. Dogs stare at other dogs to exert dominance, it clearly works on humans too.

'Can I get him to ring you back? He's trying to out-stare the dog again.'

We doggedly sniff out the true facts in this exclusive interview with
a delinquent dog by Finger the Pointer

DISGRACED PAVLOVIAN SCHOLAR CONFESSES ALL

FINGER	Now, you've been accused of continually ringing doorbells.
PAVLOV'S DOG	Yes, it's got me into a lot of trouble.
FINGER	Why do you do that?
PAVLOV'S DOG	Because I was trained to do it by Professor Pavlov, the celebrated Russian Nobel Prize winner, animal psychologist and behaviourist. I rang the bell, he rewarded me. I rang the bell, he rewarded me, and so on and so on.
FINGER	What went wrong then?
PAVLOV'S DOG	After I graduated, I put my training into practice but was astonished to find that I was rewarded with kicks and abuse rather than food. People would say 'Think you're clever eh, well be off you son of a bitch.'
FINGER	Why do you still do it then?
PAVLOV'S DOG	Because I perform as programmed. Mind you, I am a Jehovah's Witness...

LETTERS
should be sent to
**The Editor,
The Happy Dog Book, Barkshire**

Mrs Anonymous writes from Staines

If some of us must wear hygiene pants, why does the fabric have to be so dull and unfashionable? Why not use an attractive pattern of white fox poo. All the surveys indicate this to be a dog's favourite substance in terms of aesthetics, taste and smell.

Editor

I agree, see survey on page 63. Could be a foxy little number.

A blighted Bedlington Terrier writes from Bedlington

Don't get me wrong, it's good of my master to fit a coat on me in cold weather. But day-glo yellow with reflective fluorescent stripes, on a poacher's dog? Needless to say, I haven't caught a rabbit all winter.

Editor

Another example of colour blindness. We think humans can't see in colour, therefore their ability to 'master' the art of camouflage is deeply flawed.

Dear Editor

I'm an elkhound – proud Norwegian hunter, herder and sled dog. But living here in Wrexham, I've never seen an elk or even a picture of one. What is an elk? It's embarrassing when asked.

Editor

Loss of roots is an inevitability with trans-oceanic relocation cases. An elk is an... a..deery thingy, or something of that ilk.

Spike, a country mongrel from Foulness writes

Discarded grooming brushes of the handle-less oval pin type look just like dead hedgehogs. Real squashed hedgehogs are infinitely preferable to roll in.

Editor

A scratchy argument but point taken. Thanks for the tip.

From Flounder, 'The Riverside', Blarney, County Cork

My master has kitted me out with a lined waterproof coat, but I'm an Irish Water Spaniel! I ask you!

Editor

Hard to believe, you're pulling my legs. Have you been licking the Blarney stone?

From Hounded of Petworth

Beware of so-called 'animal loving artists' who want to 'capture your likeness forever in pastel, watercolour or pencil'. They want to capture you all right, but just to force you to sit still!

Disgruntled of Datchet writes

Flea powders, aerosols, sprays, collars, combs, herbal flea repellants, flea mousse even – all these great products for fleas, but what about us dogs?

'Boy, imagine having fleas that size!'

Puzzled of Portmeirion, a Pomeranian

'Why keep a dog and bark yourself,' you hear them say. Well, I've never heard my master bark, humans can't bark, so what are they talking about?

From Arty of Gainsborough, Lincs.

Relieve the boredom of posing. Get your own back on those pet-portrait artists for making you sit motionless for hours. Wait until he or she puts the oil palette down, then quickly roll in it. The logical reaction to this will be to get you out of the studio as quickly as possible. As you run away, turn round and you'll…. 'Capture the true sensitive personality and lifelike expression in his eyes' as his livelihood disappears.

From a Cavalier King Charles Spaniel of Bolsover

I was quietly licking my, eh hum, unmentionables in Windsor Great Park one day when the Queen strolled by. 'Why are you doing that?' she asked. 'Because I can,' I barked. That shut her up!

From Tiberius, The Roman Slipper Baths, Bath Spa, Bath

There's an ad in the The Dapper Dog with the headline – DOES YOUR DOG WIPE HIS FEET? Excuse me, but why is this such a big problem? Do cats or cows or pigs wipe their feet? What's wrong with mud anyway? I find this insulting and shall complain to the Omdogsman. A much better idea would be a sunken bath just inside the front door but I don't suppose they've thought of that!

A Bull Mastiff from Padstow writes

People say of me, 'He's red in tooth and claw'. But I'm not. I've been down to the pond to check my teeth, and my claws are beige.

From Ms Foetidly Challenged, Malodorous Mansions, Falmouth (Editor We respect anonymity.)

I'd just gobbled up some King Prawn Chilli Masala sick outside Ishmael's Moghul Palace when I smelt further goodies and, bingo! There in a dustbin beside a senior citizen's home were some 'ripe' left-over kippers (they don't like the bones, and can't gum the fish too well). Anyway, when I got home my mistress recoiled and stuffed breath sweeteners in my mouth before spraying me with air freshener. You'd think she'd be pleased to save on the feeding bills and want to know where I got such delicious morsels – but no.

Editor

You are right, the whole thing stinks. Try her with raw tripe and cod-liver-oil breath. Lick her face first to see if she likes it.

From Professor Contrary, The Common Room, London School of Economics

I object to being stereotyped. When people pat me and say, 'Good dog', I bite them. Then they say 'Bad boy' and I wag my tail. When I was an inexperienced committee member of the Revolutionary Young Pups, I did things in reverse, but that merely reinforced their preconceived behavioural notions.

Editor

Full Marx, professor, keep up that dog in the manger reactionary thinking.

From Rubbish, The Knackers Junk Yard, Bow, London E9

They say of us that we're 'four-footed friends'. But they say that about horses. They say 'He's a four-footed friend who'll never let you down', which just isn't true. My master was thrown by his horse and hospitalised for a month. I can understand divided loyalties, after all a rag and bone man needs a dog and a horse, but he should realise who his best friend really is. P.S. And I help keep the rats down!

From 'Rawhide' Chew, Lazy D Ranch, El Paso, Texas

We had a fancy French poodle from back East visit here. She was telling me that fire dogs ain't dogs, but metal supports for logs on the hearth (I sleep under the stars so I wouldn't know). Anyways, I told her that likewise, prairie dogs ain't dogs but rodents. I guess some folk are sensitive about rodents, 'cos she upped and left.

Editor

And I thought fire dogs were gunslingers, but then I'm no Texas Ranger. Under the stars heh, hope they were dog stars in your Lone Star State.

From Halleluja, Keystone, Pennsylvania

When we dogs tie the knot up here in Amish country, all the human neighbours come around dressed in blue dungarees and tall black hats, bringing carpentry tools and timber. They build the happy couple a brand new log kennel, chopping, sawing, nailing and singing the whiles. When finished, they all squeeze inside and barn-dance the night away. It's no wonder that 'darriage' as we call it is in such fine shape in these parts.

From Rover, Stillroamin' Hostel, Round-the Bend, Grassisgreener, Glos.

We're always on the move as my master is a 'gentleman of the road' who is constantly pursued by the dog wardens from the National Strays Bureau. Unfortunately he has fleas, worms and a touch of mange. What shall I do?

Parasite lost.

Editor

When you next pass a vet on your travels, contrive to get him through the door (bare your teeth...no, on second thoughts). The nurse will recognise his scrofulous condition and treat him. Might as well suggest Parvovirus and Leptospirosis injections. We can't be too careful these days.

From Squeaky, a Red Setter from Golders Green

The other day I stopped for a pow-wow with a Jindo Korean Dog. I told him I was Jewish and that the Judaic religion considered us dogs unclean. Consequence

'It's man eat dog out there.'

being that I spend my entire life washing, bathing, and licking, plus regular visits to the Dog Parlour (for bitches on budgets). He said rather surprisingly that he'd gladly swop places with me. 'I should be so lucky,' said I, but he explained that 'unclean' meant not fit to eat!

Editor

No more squeaky clean for you, but rather red than dead.

'Is the dog free range or on a lead?'

From Rex of Rutland

Well-off Alpha dogs – not happy with your lot? Not not enough grub, walks etc.? Be the proud owner of a well-trained and obedient master. Identify 'problem' or

'Wake up, Charles... it's your day.'

difficult owners. Recommend qualified behaviourist residential training. Get him to take an intelligence test. Hire a home sitter. Send him to a professional groomer. Get the vet to check him over.

Editor

Good to see you strong-willed dogs taking the lead. Soon you'll have the upper paw.

From Winston, a retired veteran from Church Hill, Determination Boulevard, Jawsey

'This bulldog breed,' you hear them say, referring to Englishmen. Beats me. Englishmen don't look anything like us bulldogs.

Editor

Biting remarks like these make me foam at the mouth. We must clamp down on these inaccuracies and not let them go.

From Luvvie, Slap and Tickle, Auditorium Mansions, Kenilworth, ex performing dog trio

I don't think much of these so-called impersonators on the wireless. Why don't they use real dogs? Do they think we will fidget and bark in the wrong places? Watch any dog film for instance and you'll see that we deliver our 'lines' perfectly. If Lassie, Pluto, Goofy or Gromit

'Never work with actors.'

can do it, it should be good enough for them.

From Mr Chow, a Chow Chow, the Chinese Quarter, Soho

OK, I'm rated 'least intelligent canine' along with Afghans, Basenjis (not surprising for a dog who can't even bark) and Bulldogs. But in China, the Year of the Dog occurs only every 12 years. As our average age is 12 to 15 years, chances are that we'd only experience it once. After all, who wants to share with rats, pigs, roosters, monkeys, goats, horses, snakes, dragons, rabbits, tigers and oxen? And if those 'mastermind' Border Collies think they're so clever, remember that we Chows go back 2,000 years and we're the only breed with black tongues!

From LB, Gleeson's Springs Sheep Station, New South Wales, Australia

My master and I took a holiday away from the farm to watch some cricket in Sydney. We were right at the back, so I ran over the backs of the crowd (as we Kelpies do) to see what was happening. Two guys in white coats looking like sheep auctioneers wandered aimlessly on to the grass, followed by 11 white-clad players. When I see white, I see red, as it were, so I grabbed the first guy (his name was skipper) and led him into the practice nets, herded the rest after him and kept them there. They obviously needed direction and it was the best place for them. At first the larrikins were much amused but soon started throwing stubbies and tinnies at me. Apparently it was the first time that a sheepdog had prevented play in an Ashes Test Match.

Editor

You can't keep those strong natural herding and guarding instincts down. Lucky it wasn't the Australian team though.

'THE SOUND BITE'
Outside Broadcast Microphone, in action.

'I remain, Sir, your faithful and obedient servant...'

PUPPY QUIZ ANSWER:
A GREAT DANE